SO-EAM-650

THE MICROWAVE HINT BOOK

by

CHRISTA CRAIG

ILLUSTRATIONS BY NANCY FLEMING

Copyright ©1981 by Mary Christa Craig
All rights reserved

Published by Microwave Kitchen Press
Post Office Box 17466
Pittsburgh, PA 15235

Thank you to my encouraging friend Barbara Stout, my family and Nancy Fleming, for invaluable help, generously given.

The hints in this book are suggested techniques and supplementary recommendations for efficient microwave cooking. The author cannot guarantee total success. An owner should refer to individual manufacturer's manuals for usage and care.

Contents

Contents

Introduction

Congratulations! You own or have serious interest in an efficient microwave oven. Now what?

As a new microwave cook, you will find patience is a great virtue. The first weeks of cooking can be discouraging. This book is designed to provide basic hints clearly and as simply as possible. You must experiment and learn important techniques, remembering that disasters happen in all cooking methods.

The following pages are full of tips acquired during many years of teaching microwave classes and seminars. Students have helped by telling me their experiences. I hope valuable time will be saved by following these guides and short-cuts.

THE MICROWAVE HINT BOOK contains first-hand information and reliable favorite recipes. The text is presented concisely, truthfully and with a bit of humor.

Now you have it - use it! Slow and easy, one Micro-step at a time.

"Diamonds and gold, I do not crave;
all I want is a microwave."

Busy Lady

HELPFUL HINTS FOR PURCHASING

Purchase a microwave oven when you have time to learn to use it. This is a completely new method of cooking and needs dedicated effort. It is best to buy an oven in advance of holidays or special cooking celebrations. The woman who unwraps a surprise microwave on Christmas morning and feels obligated to create a perfect meal for 14 that afternoon, is the person who hates it forever more. She ends the day crying in her eggnog.

OH! FOR ME!!
A MICROWAVE OVEN!!

Please don't present elderly family members with a microwave gift to "make life easier." After 60 years of conventional cooking, many people have difficulty changing style. Classes are filled with motivated but guilty octogenarians who are reluctant to admit they dislike a Mother's Day gift.

A microwave oven is an expensive investment. Do your research and microwave homework well before a purchase. Talk to a friend who owns one and inquire about useful features. Read manuals, take an introductory class and consider renting a microwave.

3

Put your oven in a convenient location. Is your kitchen too small? A microwave cart is a solution to limited space. A microwave can be set on wall shelves. Models are available that fit over a range and include an exhaust fan. Owners enjoy the flexibility of a microwave. Use it in the family room for parties, the diningroom for warm-ups, the patio for picnics and take the microwave on vacation. (You may need someone from Rent-a-Weight Lifter to heft it around).

WHAT TO LOOK FOR WHEN BUYING

When it comes to microwaves, simple is best. You need efficient, speedy, clean and cool cooking. The same flavor, nutritious product and food quality is available in a $300 or $600 microwave unit. Your money is buying features, not a difference in cooking ability.

To paraphrase Will Rogers, "I have never met a microwave I didn't like." Basically, each manufacturers produces a unit equal to each other and they are all good.

Features will range from simple one power ovens to sophisticated sensors and memories. Experience tells me that the most important feature is: At least four variable power levels. This feature enables energy settings for a variety of foods. The basic important levels are HIGH (100%), MEDIUM HIGH (70%), MEDIUM (50%) and defrost (30%). A microwave containing just 1 or 2 power levels often limits an owner to reheating and defrosting.

A second desirable and useful feature is a temperature probe. A probe registers the internal temperature of food and is used in place of time cooking. The microwave shuts off automatically when the desired preset food temperature is reached. This feature is an asset when cooking large roasts, casseroles and for reheating.

Question the salesperson carefully. They should explain the reasons why added features would be practical in your circumstances. Often, features such as

4

multiple memories and computerized instructions are useful in a limited number of cooking situations.

Keep it simple and you will probably save money and be perfectly satisfied.

IS A MICROWAVE SAFE?

Yes. Under Federal law, the government sets stringent safety standards to which all microwave manufacturers comply. Underwriters Laboratories test prototypes of microwaves against the government and other safety standards. They perform inspections and quality control tests to assure proper operation.

For safety and best results, always follow the manufacturer's instructions.

I have met only two "micro-fools" who defied safety precautions and used the oven for purposes other than cooking. One lady blew up six clay pots trying to simulate a kiln. The other gentlemen, returning from a successful hunting trip, stuffed small antlers, a rabbit skin and his boots into the microwave to dry. The antlers cracked, the rabbit skin became tough leather, and the boots developed a permanent ripe odor.

"Tomorrow, I have to quit procrastinating and learn to really cook in my microwave."

Typical Owner

HOW DOES IT WORK?

Microwaves are very short radio-frequency waves. Your oven is similar to a little broadcasting station. Electrical energy is converted to microwave energy by a power source called a magnetron tube. The moisture molecules located in food absorb this energy and rub rapidly together causing friction. This friction produces instant heat and cooking.

5

No Honey, there are no microwaves in your tummy!!

FOODS COOK FROM THE INSIDE OUT — RIGHT or WRONG?

Wrong! The microwaves penetrate the surface of the food about 1 to 1- 3/4 inches, depending on the type and density of food. Heat from the vibrating mole- cules moves from the outer surface toward the middle of the food, cooking merrily along the way. This heating reaction is called conduction or transference.

TIMING IS THE MOST IMPORTANT FACTOR IN MICROWAVE COOKING!

TIMING IS THE MOST IMPORTANT FACTOR IN MICROWAVE COOKING!

Your eyesight is not failing. The sentence is repeated because it is so critical. Cooking technique and timing are more serious than the content of the recipe. Timing depends on many variables such as the amount, moisture content, shape and density of food.

"I asked my neighbor, who loves her microwave, what to expect in the beginning. She said with a laugh, "Expect to mess it up, Pal."

Microwave Student

WHAT TO DO?

WHAT CAN I EXPECT?

Your greatest initial problem may be overcooking. Also, microwave food produces its own characteristics and may appear different from a conventional recipe. In some ways, you may have to learn cooking techniques all over again.

If you use the oven for defrosting and reheating only, the basic methods will be quickly learned. But, if you totally embrace this culinary concept and decide to use the oven to the fullest – you need time. Expect to eventually use the microwave for 75% to 85% of your cooking needs.

"The elderly man asked if eating microwave food would renew his romantic vigor. I said "What the heck, Sir, try it."

Microwave Salesman

7

ARE NEW DISHES NEEDED?

Eventually one may wish to purchase an important item but meanwhile save money by discovering the resources available. You may have a house full of suitable accessories. Use platters, mixing bowls, salad or punch bowls and sea shells. I retrieved an old bean pot and a plastic colander from the sandbox. They both work well besides adding a unique gritty texture to the food. One friend claims her favorite 3-quart casserole is her Grandmother's chamber pot. Use your imagination looking for a variety of microwave-proof dishes. The perfect dish may be hiding in the attic or perhaps, under the bed.

WHAT UTENSILS CAN BE USED IN A MICROWAVE?

- Paper products such as towels, napkins, cardboard cartons and hot drink cups.

- Plastic foam plates and cups for short-term heating. (Melting can occur when used with high fat foods).

- Use wood and straw dishes for quick reheating. Wooden tools that can be left in the microwave for frequent stirring.

- Dinnerware, ceramics and porcelain, Pyrex products and pottery without metal trim or handles.

- Special Microwave plastic such as Anchor Hocking, Mister Microwave, Nupac and many others. Look for signs stating "Microwave Safe" or "Suitable for Microwave" when purchasing new utensils.

- Do not use metal pots, pans, foil-lined trays, metal-trimmed dishes, conventional thermometers or metal skewers.

* * Note * *

WHEN IN DOUBT, TEST DISHES. PLACE THE EMPTY DISH IN THE OVEN ALONG WITH 1 CUP WATER IN A GLASS CUP. MICRO-WAVE ON HIGH - 1 MINUTE. IF DISH IS TOO HOT TO TOUCH, DON'T USE IT. A WARM DISH CAN BE USED FOR SHORT-TERM COOKING. A COOL DISH IS SAFE FOR EVERYDAY MICROWAVE COOKING.

CAN METAL PANS BE USED?

No. Microwaves pass through glass, plastic and cera-mic and are transmitted into the food. Metal reflects and is not transparent to microwaves. Because the waves do not penetrate metal, no energy is available to heat food.

The exception to the rule is foil and low aluminum (foil) trays. Small, smooth pieces of aluminum foil can be used for shielding vulnerable areas from over-cooking. Foil is useful when defrosting. Placing foil over thawed sections, allows the remaining frozen portion to keep defrosting. Use small pieces of foil and don't let it touch the sides or top of the micro-wave.

"I feel the settlement was fair. She received the car, I got the microwave."
California Paper

WHAT ARE THE MOST ESSENTIAL DISHES?

Do buy a meat trivet or roasting rack to suspend meat out of the juices. A microwave trivet is usually slotted, fits in it's own dish or may be placed in another baking dish. This utensil can usually be used as a bacon rack.

My favorite dish is a 8-inch round 2-quart cake pan with high sides. This pan holds half of a large cake mix and allows for increased cake volume. When not baking, it can be an all-purpose dish.

A 10-cup glass measuring cup, called a batter bowl is great for pasta, soup and candy.

Rings molds or round baking pans with holes in the center are recommended for meat loaves, cakes and casseroles.

OTHER FREQUENTLY USED DISHES

° Muffin or cupcake holders made of microwave-proof plastic.
° A 12 x 8 inch flat dish (called a utility dish).
° Round glass dishes ranging in size from 12 ounces to 5 quarts. A 5-quart casserole is usually the largest dish to fit in the oven and is useful for quantity cooking.
° Custard and glass measuring cups.
° A microwave browning dish or grill.

WHAT FACTORS EFFECT COOKING?

The whole subject of microwave cooking would be so much easier if only firm and fool-proof rules existed. Since these rules aren't available, cooks must be aware of the following principles.

Quantity of Food

Small amounts will cook and heat faster than larger volumes. As the food is increased, so is the time it takes to cook.

Starting Temperatures

The colder the food, the longer it will take to cook. Refrigerated foods will need more time and microwave energy to reach doneness than if started at room temperature.

Size and Shape

Microwave foods, just like people, are more desirable when evenly shaped. Thin areas cook faster than thick. Several foods cooked together, like stew or soup, should be similar in size and shape. A round, compact roast will be easier to cook than a bulky leg of lamb. Uneven corners and protruding portions found in roasts and poultry need small pieces of smooth foil for shielding. Cover these areas to minimize over-exposure to microwave energy.

Density

Light weight, porous foods like bread will cook and heat faster than dense, compact items such as potatoes.

Arrangement of Food

Arrange thick, dense food to the outside of the dish. Foods cook quickly at the outer edges of the container and slower in the center. Place similar sized foods such as cupcakes and potatoes in a hollow circle with 1 inch between.

Dish Shape

Round shaped dishes and ring casseroles allow even microwave penetration. A large, flat and shallow container will cook the same amount of food faster than a deeper dish of the same capacity. More surface area is exposed to microwaves in the low dish, heating faster.

* * Note * *

Microwave cooking takes longer at a higher altitude.
Follow directions given on packages for altitude ad-
justment. Start recipes at recommended time and generally, add 1 minute cooking time for each 5 minutes
of microwave time.

*"I decorated a party cake with pretty microwave-dried
roses. They looked delicious but it was a dumb idea
because 2 guests ate them."*

Creative Cook

WHAT IS A POWER LEVEL?

Variable power levels are similar to heat controls in
conventional cooking. Power settings regulate heat
energy allowing for a choice and are measured by the
percentage of total time the energy is activated.

The recipes in this book use four power settings available on most models. If your oven does not have variable powers, most of the recipes can still be utilized.
Recipes will need more watching, turning or stirring
and times may vary.

HIGH POWER (100%) Full power used for quick cooking
of foods that can tolerate fast cooking with intense
heat and contain high moisture content. Generally is
used for boiling liquids, cooking vegetables, fruits,
fish and candy.

MEDIUM HIGH (70%) Provides slightly less energy and
is used to heat frozen food, baked goods and pasta.
This power is often the choice for heating previously
cooked foods.

MEDIUM (50%) Half power used for meat cookery, giving
a longer cooking time for added tenderizing and flavor.
Also used to cook custard and custard-base desserts.

DEFROST (30%) Used to defrost frozen foods and cook
delicate foods. One-third power used to simmer, stew
and for drying fruits and vegetables.

12

A good idea is to test the cooking time required in your unit against the suggested recipe times in this cookbook.

To test: Place 1 cup room temperature water in oven. Microwave on
High until bubbles break the water
surface. Water should boil in 2-1/2
to 3 minutes in a 625 watt unit. If
the time is significantly shorter or
longer, expect recipes to correspond
accordingly.

All recipes that appear in the
Microwave Hint Book have been
developed and tested using 600
to 700 watt microwave units.
If you have a 400 to 500 watt
unit, add 30 seconds to each
minute of cooking time. If
you have a 500 to 600 watt
unit, add 15 seconds to each
minute of cooking time.

*"Bachelors are the most satisfied microwave cooks.
They are so proud of their new-found cooking abili-
ties, they don't recognize a disaster."*

Cooking Instructor

ARE THERE SECRETS TO SUCCESSFUL RECIPE CONVERSION?

° Converting and adapting recipes is not complicated
  once you understand the techniques of microwaving.

° Begin by considering the food – can it be successfully microwaved? Certain items such as yeast
  breads, souffles, and deep-fried food are best prepared conventionally. Look in a microwave cookbook
  for a recipe similar in moisture, amount of food,
  power level and technique.

13

Hints To Remember Are:

° Liquids do not evaporate in a microwave. Moisture content is important. Reduce liquid in some recipes by 1/4. When making gravy, casseroles and puddings, you may wish to add more thickening agent.

° Use 1/4 less seasoning. Lack of evaporation and shorter cooking times intensify the flavors.

° Count on shorter cooking time. The average food requires 1/4 the conventional cooking time. This is not a firm rule as some foods take less or more time depending on the amount and type of food.

I CAN TRY IT AGAIN - IT'S FAST ENOUGH!

° Reduce or eliminate those fattening cooking oils when frying and sautéing. Remove excess grease from recipe during cooking. Who needs it!

° "Carry-over" cooking is a factor in conversion. Remove foods just before being completely done to be safe.

° Foods high in fats and sugars absorb energy, get very hot and cook quickly.

DON'T GIVE UP IF A FAVORITE CONVENTIONAL RECIPE FLOPPED THE FIRST TIME. Try again!

14

WHEN AND WHAT DO I COVER?

A cover promotes steaming, leaving foods moist and tender. In most cases, food that is conventionally cooked with a cover will also be tightly covered in a microwave. Tightly cover foods with a lid or sealed plastic wrap to speed cooking and seal in the heat.

Plastic wrap is a convenient covering for airtight seals. It should be pleated or slashed to allow steam to expand. Get in the habit of opening covers and plastic wrap <u>away from you</u>. Steam escapes quickly and you can receive a "nasty" burn.

"Cover lightly" refers to a loose, partial covering of waxed paper or parchment paper. It holds in some moisture and heat without complete steaming.

I USE PARCHMENT OR FREEZER PAPER IN PLACE OF WAXED PAPER. PARCHMENT PAPER HOLDS SHAPE, CAN BE WIPED OFF AND REUSED TIME AFTER TIME. IT DOESN'T BECOME SOGGY AND FALL IN THE FOOD.

Porous covering such as paper towels and napkins absorb moisture and eliminate spattering. They prevent soggy sandwiches by keeping bread surfaces dry and are ideal for cooking bacon.

Boil and oven-proof plastic bags hold in moisture and help tenderize foods. Useful for roasts, whole poultry and less tender cuts of meat. I like plastic oven bags for long, slow cooking with a minimum amount of liquid. Beware of using metal twists for closing and be sure the bags are heat proof. Once I cooked a hot dog in a plain plastic sandwich bag. The bag melted and completely disappeared. What a shock!

All plastic cooking bags should be slashed or pierced.

Try using everyday dishes such as saucers or dinner plates as lids.

DO I HAVE TO STIR AND ROTATE FOOD?

Uneven cooking can result when foods are not occasionally moved or stirred. Stir from the outside edges to the center. Rotate dishes that can not be stirred, 1/4 to 1/2 turn during microwaving. Recipes usually include instructions. It is possible to overstir. Recently, I read a recipe for a 3-minute sauce which called for stirring every 20 seconds. I was curious as to when it cooked.

"I was microwaving a 12 lb. turkey. As a joke, my children substituted a 1 lb. Cornish Hen in the dish. Upon opening the door - for an instant, I truly believed the microwave had shrunk that bird."

Harried Housewife

STANDING TIME MAKES FOR ACCURACY

Microwave food needs a "standing time" as it will continue to cook after the oven shuts off. The carry over or residual cooking is due to high heat in the food which continues to increase and equalize during the setting period. This factor is vital because over-cooking tends to toughen, dry out and harden food. Because overcooked food can not be revitalized, it is often wise to undercook and underthaw food slightly and let it stand.

IF FOOD IS GETTING HARD - YOU ARE OVERCOOKING AND NOT TAKING ADVANTAGE OF STANDING TIME.

"Grandma, you can't get the television show by pushing button "5". That's the microwave!"

Grandchild

HOW IS A MEAL PLANNED?

Microwave the foods needing the longest cooking and standing time first. These items such as roasts, casseroles and large poultry can be cooked early in the day and reheated. Microwave the shorter cooking and standing time dishes such as vegetables, fish, eggs, an fruit closer to serving time. Last minute items include bread and rolls, drinks and quick reheats. Think through the cooking requirements and sequence. Try preparing ahead to avoid being backed up with 3 or 4 last minute dishes. Microwave meal planning does take practice!

"Plastic wrap is brought to you by the same people who make fly-paper"

Tightly Wrapped Lady

CAN I COOK A WHOLE MEAL AT ONCE?

It is difficult to coordinate a complete meal combination. Time savings are minimal since additional foods mean increased cooking time.

A microwave shelf or rack is designed to help utilize all the space available in your oven. Shelf instructions talk about complete meal preparation. It is tricky to achieve. On the positive side, shelves are very useful when utilized for reheating several items. You can never cook for an army in a microwave, but quantity reheating is convenient. Up to four foods can be heated successfully at one time.

"It sits on the counter, all shiny and new. Now - what in the world do I do?"

Puzzled Peggy

WHAT IS A BROWNING DISH?

A browning dish enables you to sear, brown, grill and fry food. The ceramic dish has a special oxide coating on the bottom which absorbs microwave energy and  becomes <u>very</u> hot. The empty dish is placed in the oven for preheating. Food is added and browns quickly on the first side. When food is turned over or stirred, the second side will be lightly seared. Foods will not be fried to the same degree of crispness expected with conventional cooking, but is quite adequate. Steaks, chops, grilled sandwiches, eggs and stir-fried vegetables are suggested foods to be cooked on a browning dish or grill.

IS A BROWNING DISH NECESSARY?

A browning dish greatly expands the types of food one can prepare in a microwave. I tell owners to postpone the use of a browning dish for a month or two after purchasing a unit. With so many new things to learn, concentrating on mastering browning dish techniques can muddle a mind. After gaining confidence and learning to "think microwave," then expand to this helpful and convenient accessory.

"Remember, a microwave is a steam-cooker."

18

HOW ABOUT MICROWAVING FROZEN TV DINNERS?

Foods can be cooked in foil trays up to 3/4 inch deep. Remove the foil lid and replace the tray in its box or cover with plastic wrap. You may eventually learn to like the slightly icy bottoms on the TV dinners. (remember microwaves don't penetrate through metal) Small TV dinners cooked on High take 5 to 7 minutes. Large trays need 12 to 15 minutes.

The best method is to transfer the food to a dinner plate and cover tightly. Frozen dinner food on a dish heats quickly in 3 to 5 minutes on High. Porous foods, dough, cakes, puddings and french fries in a frozen dinner should be cooked conventionally.

WHAT ARE THE ELECTRICAL SPARKS THAT SOMETIMES FLY A-ROUND INSIDE THE MICROWAVE?

Beware of metal twisters and hidden metal wires (some cups contain metal reinforcement in the handles). Certain types of metal can cause "arcing." The sparks and clicking sound accompanying arcing warns that something is in the oven that shouldn't be there. Take it out and the sparks will stop. Arcing is a rare occurance, if directions are followed, but it can scare your ears off.

"The kids were tossing around a new brown frisbee. In reality, the frisbee was a round batch of overcooked brownies."

Microwave Mother

WHAT RECIPES ARE BEST AND SAFEST FOR CHILDREN WHO WISH TO BEGIN MICROWAVING?

Recipes cooked only a few minutes are usually safe because the dishes do not become hot. Urge the kids to use pot holders. Children can start cooking hot dogs and Muffin Pizzas (page 36). Quick cereals, baked apples (page 111) and fudge (page 109) are easy. Snack cakes, muffins or brownies are successful and give a child confidence to try other dishes.

BOOK BUYING TIPS

Check the copyright date before purchasing a microwave book. Books with a copyright before 1977 often do not include variable powers in recipes.

Some books are translations of foreign manufacturer's manuals and may be difficult to understand. Read a few recipes and check for power level information before purchasing.

* APPETIZERS AND ENTERTAINING *

° The guests can have fun microwaving their own snacks. Prepare party food early in the day and place it on paper plates or serving dishes.

° Think ahead! Freeze party dips and appetizers. Defrost and cook at party time.

° Why is my meatball blue? Because the blue plastic toothpick on which it is sitting melted. Plain wooden toothpicks and skewers can be placed in food before cooking. Avoid plastic and colored toothpicks which can melt and run.

° Dishwashing is no fun! Place canapes and appetizers on paper towels, plates and napkins for easy cleanup.

° The best way to evenly cook individual pieces of food such as canapes, mushrooms and meatballs is in a hollow circle.

° Please don't curdle the dip. Spreads, dips and hors d'oeuvres containing mayonnaise, sour cream and natural cheese should be microwaved on Medium power to prevent separating and curdling.

° Yogurt doesn't like heat. If you must warm yogurt, use the defrost cycle for a short period of time.

° Crackers soggy? Place stale crackers, chips or other salty snacks on a plate. Refresh on High for 45 seconds to 1 minute. Let stand for a few minutes until crisp.

21

° Warm shelled nuts for a few seconds in the microwave before chopping. It will bring out the nut oils for flavor.

° Shellfish can be steamed in their shells. Twelve clams are cooked on Medium for 3 to 4 minutes or until shells partially open. Clams that do not open are bad and should be thrown out. Serve with melted butter and lemon.

° Fast canapes are made by spreading cheese or meat salads on crackers or toasted bread. Microwave for a few seconds.

OLD ENGLISH DIP

POWER LEVEL: MEDIUM   SERVES: 1-1/2 cups
TOTAL COOKING TIME: 6 to 8 minutes
                     Temperature Probe 130°

---

2 jars (5 oz. each) sharp Old English cheese
   spread, softened
1 package (8 oz.) cream cheese, softened
1/3 cup of beer
1 tsp. Worcestershire sauce
5 to 6 drops hot pepper sauce (optional)
3 strips bacon, cooked and crumbled

Stir together cheeses, beer, Worcestershire sauce and pepper sauce in a 1-1/2 quart casserole. Microwave on Medium for 6 to 8 minutes. Add crumbled bacon and stir until smooth. Serve with salt snacks or crackers.

VARIATION:
CHEESE RAREBIT: Increase beer to 3/4 cup. At end of Microwaving time, blend 1 beaten egg and 1/2 tsp. dry mustard into cheese mixture. Microwave 1 to 2 minutes on Medium. Serve over toast. Sprinkle with paprika.

STUFFED MUSHROOMS

POWER LEVEL: HIGH   SERVES: 16 to 20 mushrooms
TOTAL COOKING TIME: 2-1/2 to 3-1/2 minutes per plate

Choose 16 to 20 medium or large firm, fresh mushrooms.
Wash and remove stems. Prepare stuffing recipe and
mound into mushroom caps. Arrange 8 to 10 mushrooms
in a circle on a round plate lined with waxed paper.
Microwave on High 2-1/2 to 3-1/2 minutes, rotating
dish after 1 minute. Repeat for remaining mushrooms.
Do not overcook or mushrooms will lose shape.

SPINACH STUFFING - Combine 1 package (10 oz.) thawed
spinach souffle, with 1 cup dry bread crumbs and 1/4
cup Parmesan cheese.

CLAM OR OYSTER STUFFING - Combine 1 package (3 oz.)
softened cream cheese, 1 can (5 oz.) clams or oysters
drained and minced with 1 Tbsp. parsley and 1/2 tsp.
minced onion. Mound into caps and sprinkle with crumbled bacon or nuts.

CREAMY SEAFOOD DIP

POWER LEVEL: MEDIUM   SERVES: 2 cups
TOTAL COOKING TIME: 4 to 5 minutes

---

1 package (8 oz.) cream cheese, softened
1 can (7 oz.) shrimp or crabmeat, rinsed and drained
1 tsp. catsup
1 tsp. horseradish
1 tsp. instant minced onion
1 tsp. Worcestershire sauce

Mix cream cheese, shrimp or crabmeat, catsup, horseradish, minced onion and Worcestershire sauce in a 1
to 1-1/2 quart casserole. Cover tightly. Microwave
on Medium for 4 to 5 minutes. Stir once during cooking. Mix well.

23

BUTTERFLY WIENERS

POWER LEVEL: HIGH   SERVES: 8 to 10
TOTAL COOKING TIME: 4 to 5 minutes

1 pound wieners
2 cups barbecue sauce

Cut wieners in 3 pieces. Slit the ends of each piece twice lengthwise in a cross shape, leaving a 1/4 inch join in the center. Place sauce in a 1-1/2 quart low dish and cover with waxed paper. Microwave on High 1 to 2 minutes. Place toothpicks in wiener pieces and add to sauce. Microwave 3 minutes on High until ends of wieners open and flair out.

CRUNCHY CHICKEN WINGS

POWER LEVEL: MEDIUM HIGH   SERVES: 24 pieces
TOTAL COOKING TIME: 10-1/2 to 12-1/2 minutes per 12
                        pieces

1/4 cup butter or margarine
1 dozen chicken wings
1/2 cup seasoned dry bread crumbs
3 Tbsp. finely chopped nuts
1/2 tsp. salt
Paprika

Place butter in a 12 x 8 baking dish. Microwave on High for 30 seconds or until melted. Cut wings at joints, separating each into 3 sections. Tip sections can be used later for soup. Combine crumbs, nuts and salt in another dish. Dip wing sections in butter and coat with crumbs. Place half of wings in baking dish with small ends toward the center. Sprinkle with paprika. Microwave on Medium High for 10 to 12 minutes or until tender. Rotate dish 1/2 turn after 5 minutes. Repeat for remaining pieces.

ROQUEFORT CHEESE MEATBALLS

POWER LEVEL: HIGH   SERVES: 14 to 16 meatballs
TOTAL COOKING TIME: 6 to 8 minutes

---

1 pound ground chuck beef   1 egg
1/2 cup fine bread crumbs   3/4 tsp. salt
2 tsp. onion, finely chopped   1/8 tsp. pepper
1/3 cup crumbled Roquefort cheese
1 Tbsp. Worcestershire sauce or 1 Tbsp. Red Wine

Mix together all ingredients. Shape into 14 to 16
balls and arrange in a circle on a 10" pie plate or
platter. Cover with waxed paper. Microwave on High
6 to 8 minutes or until no longer pink. Rearrange
meatballs halfway through cooking. Serve hot on
toothpicks.

HAM APPETIZER KABOBS

POWER LEVEL: HIGH   SERVES: 16 appetizers
TOTAL COOKING TIME: 5 to 6 minutes

---

1 pound ham, cooked and cut into 1-inch cubes
1 large green pepper, cut into 1/2-inch squares
1-1/2 cups pineapple chunks, drained
1 cup apricot preserves
1/4 cup orange juice
1/2 tsp. cinnamon or ginger
16 (4 to 5 inch) wooden skewers

Alternate ham, green pepper and pineapple chunks on 16
skewers. Place horizontally in a 2-quart baking dish.
Mix together apricot preserves, orange juice and spice.
Brush kabobs with sauce and Microwave on High for 5 to
6 minutes or until ham is warm. Turn skewers and baste
twice during cooking.

SEASONED VEGETABLES

POWER LEVEL: HIGH   SERVES: 6 servings per plate
TOTAL COOKING TIME: 10 to 13 minutes for each dish

1/4 cup butter or margarine
1/2 tsp. onion salt
1/4 tsp. parsley
1 pound fresh broccoli
1 small head cauliflower
2 medium zucchini
2 tomatoes, cut into wedges
1/4 cup Parmesan cheese

In a 1 cup measure or small bowl, combine butter, onion salt and parsley. Microwave on High for 1 minute until melted. Set aside.

Trim and cut broccoli and cauliflower into florets. Arrange florets alternately around the edge of two 10 or 12-inch serving dishes. Fill center of the dish with sliced zucchini. Cover with plastic wrap.

Microwave each plate on High for 9 to 11 minutes. Vegetables should be almost tender. Drain off any excess liquid. Arrange tomato wedges on dish and pour butter mixture over vegetables. Sprinkle with Parmesan cheese.

Microwave uncovered on High for 1 to 2 minutes. Repeat instructions with second plate. Serve with toothpicks or as finger food.

Other vegetables can be used such as partially precooked carrots, summer squash, canned beets and canned potatoes.

* HOT BEVERAGES *

° Microwave hot drinks in glasses, pottery cups, paper hot cups, plastic foam cups and serving pitchers which do not contain metal trim. Drinks can be heated in an open carton.

° Don't bother reheating a whole pot of coffee! Store coffee and tea, covered, in the refrigerator. Reheat in individual cups.

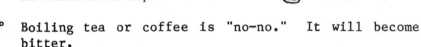

° Boiling tea or coffee is "no-no." It will become bitter.

° Arrange cups in a circle with an inch of space between each cup. No cup sitting in the middle of the circle, please. Place all the cups on a glass dish or tray for easy removal.

° Avoid bubble, bubble, toil and trouble. Before adding an instant mix to boiling water, wait 30 seconds. The mixture will not boil up and spill.

° It takes a cup of water 2-1/2 to 3 minutes to boil. (Remember that cold liquids take longer to boil)

              Average heating time on High Power

        1 cup   1 to 1-1/2 minutes
        2 cups   2 minutes
        4 cups   4 minutes

° Don't cry over spilled milk! Milk boils over quickly in a microwave.

° When heating milk-base liquids use Medium High (70%) Water-base beverages are heated on High (100%)

° Using a temperature probe? Milk-base beverages are heated to 130°F. Water-base liquids are heated to 150° - 160°F.

° Heat a glass or snifter of wine or brandy for a royal aroma.   27

HOT TODDY

POWER LEVEL: HIGH   SERVES: 1 cup
TOTAL COOKING TIME: 2 to 3 minutes

---

1 Tbsp. sugar
3/4 cup water
1/4 tsp. lemon juice
2 oz. light or dark rum
1 tsp. butter
Nutmeg
Cinnamon stick

Combine sugar, water, lemon juice and rum in a mug.
Microwave on High 2 to 2-1/2 minutes or until steaming
hot. Float butter on top, sprinkle with nutmeg and
serve with cinnamon stick for stirring.

RUSSIAN TEA

POWER LEVEL: HIGH   SERVES: 60
TOTAL COOKING TIME: 1 to 1-1/2 minutes

---

1 cup powdered orange flavored drink
1 cup sugar
1 package (3 oz.) lemonade mix
1 cup instant tea
1 tsp. cinnamon
1 tsp. ground cloves
1/2 tsp. ground allspice

Mix ingredients well. Store in an airtight container.
To make one cup of Russian Tea: Microwave one cup of
water on High for 1 to 1-1/2 minutes. Stir in 2 teaspoons of tea mix.

HOT TOMATO COCKTAIL

POWER LEVEL: HIGH   SERVES: 6 to 8
TOTAL COOKING TIME: 10 to 12 minutes

4 cups tomato juice
1 cup water
1/2 cup packed celery leaves
1/4 cup diced onion
1/2 tsp. salt
1/2 tsp. sugar
2 Tbsp. lemon juice
1/4 tsp. pepper
1/4 tsp. Worcestershire sauce
1 tsp. horseradish

Combine all ingredients in 2-quart glass dish. Microwave on High 10 to 12 minutes or until steaming hot but
not boiling. Strain before serving.

MULLED CIDER

POWER LEVEL: HIGH   SERVES: 4 to 5
TOTAL COOKING TIME: 5 to 7 minutes

1 quart apple cider
4 whole cloves
2 sticks cinnamon
1/4 cup rum (optional)
1/2 orange, thinly sliced with peel
3 Tbsp. sugar
3 whole allspice

In 1-1/2 quart container combine all ingredients except
rum. Microwave on High 5 to 7 minutes or until steaming hot. Stir halfway through cooking time. If using
rum, add during last minute of cooking time. Strain if
desired. Serve while cider is steaming.

NOTES_____

A WHOLE PAGE!
FOR MY MICRO-NOTES!

* SOUP *

° Heat soup in a mug or serving bowl.

° When using a temperature probe, heat milk-base soups to 140° - 150°. Water-base soups heat to 160° - 170°.

° Dehydrated soups sometimes take longer to cook and become rehydrated. Best to cook soups with dehydrated noodles and rice on Medium. Let stand, covered a few minutes before serving.

° "My soup makes exploding sounds." Stir the soup or set it at a slightly lower power setting to stop the pop.

° Heat canned soups with a cover. One cup heats in 2 to 3 minutes. One quart heats in 7 to 8 minutes.

° Start "soups from scratch" in a large bowl to prevent boil-overs.

° Add a package of dehydrated chicken soup to chicken stock to make it more flavorful. A bouillon cube is good, also.

° Save soup stock. Freeze in a 1-cup container, defrost in microwave and add to casseroles.

° Cook water-base homemade soups with a tight cover. Milk-base homemade soups are microwaved without a lid.

° Trim the fat from meat before adding to soup to prevent the "greasy's."

31

FRENCH ONION SOUP

POWER LEVEL: HIGH   SERVES: 6 to 8
TOTAL COOKING TIME: 18 to 20 minutes

---

3 Tbsp. butter or margarine
4 large onions, thinly sliced
3 cans (10-1/2 oz.) condensed beef broth
3 cups water
French bread slices, toasted, or croutons
Grated Parmesan cheese

Combine butter and onions in a 3-quart casserole. Cover
tightly. Microwave on High for 8 minutes or until
onions are transparent, stirring once.

Stir in broth and water. Cover tightly. Microwave on
High 10 to 14 minutes or until onions are tender and
soup is hot. Garnish with bread and cheese.

TUNA CORN CHOWDER

POWER LEVEL: MEDIUM HIGH   SERVES: 6 to 8
TOTAL COOKING TIME: 16 to 18 minutes

---

1 can (12 oz.) mexicorn, drained
1 can (16-1/2 oz.) cream-style corn
1 can (10-3/4 oz.) cream of potato soup
1 Tbsp. minced onion
3/4 tsp. celery salt
1 tsp. Worcestershire sauce
Dash pepper
1 can (6-1/2 oz.) tuna, drained
2-1/2 cups milk

In a 2-1/2 quart casserole, combine all ingredients -
mix well. Cover tightly and Microwave on Medium High
for 16 to 18 minutes. Stir once halfway through
cooking. Serve hot.

MUSHROOM SOUP

POWER LEVEL: HIGH AND MEDIUM   SERVES: 4
TOTAL COOKING TIME: 11 to 14 minutes

---

2 cups (8 oz.) fresh mushrooms, sliced
1 Tbsp. chopped onion
1/4 cup butter or margarine
1/4 cup flour
1 Tbsp. beef bouillon granules
2 cups water
2 Tbsp. dry white wine (optional)
1 cup half and half cream

In a 1-1/2 quart casserole, combine mushrooms, onion and butter. Microwave, uncovered, on High for 3 to 4 minutes until mushrooms are just tender. Stir once during cooking. Add flour bouillon granules and water. Microwave, uncovered, on High 6 to 8 minutes, until mixture boils and thickens. Stir twice during cooking. Stir in wine and cream. Microwave on Medium 2 minutes until heated.

POTATO SOUP

POWER LEVEL: HIGH   SERVES: 4 to 6
TOTAL COOKING TIME: 25 to 27 minutes

---

3 cups potatoes, cut in 1/2 inch cubes
1/4 cup onions, chopped
1/4 cup celery, chopped
1/2 cup water   1-1/2 cups milk
1 tsp. salt   1 cup chicken broth or bouillon
2 Tbsp. flour   1 Tbsp. parsley, chopped

Combine potatoes, onion, celery, water and salt in a 2-quart casserole. Cover tightly. Microwave on High 10 to 12 minutes or until vegetables are tender. Blend flour, milk, chicken broth and parsley until smooth. Stir into vegetables. Microwave on High 15 minutes until thick. Stir every 5 minutes.

VEGETABLE BEEF SOUP

POWER LEVEL: HIGH   SERVES: 4 to 6
TOTAL COOKING TIME: 26 to 30 minutes

---

1 pound lean ground beef
1/4 cup onion, chopped
1 cup potatoes, peeled and cut in 1/4 inch cubes
1 cup cabbage, shredded
1 package (10 oz.) frozen mixed vegetables
1 can (16 oz.) tomatoes, including liquid
2 beef bouillon cubes
3 cups hot water
1 Tbsp. Worcestershire sauce
1 Tbsp. parsley flakes
1/2 tsp. salt

Crumble beef into a 4-quart casserole. Add onion, potatoes and cabbage. Cover tightly. Microwave on High
6 to 8 minutes until meat is browned, stirring once.
Drain and break up meat. Add remaining ingredients
and mix thoroughly. Cover tightly and Microwave on
High 20 to 22 minutes or until potatoes are tender.
Let stand, covered, 10 minutes to blend flavors.

NOTE: 1-1/2 cups cooked cubed beef may be substituted
for ground beef. Eliminate first step in directions
when using cooked meat.

* SANDWICHES *

° Beware! Bread is porous and heats quickly. Overheated bread becomes tough and hard. A whole loaf
of bread, heated over three minutes can be used as
a football.

° Heat rolls and bread until they feel
"just warm." Conventional-type, pi-
ping hot bread is not possible.

° Fast food freak? Sandwiches can be reheated in
carry-out containers if they are not foiled-lined.

° The best way to heat sandwiches is in paper towels
or napkins to absorb excess moisture.

° Soggy sandwiches? Try
toasting your sandwich
bread. Toast bread in
advance, cool and cover
tightly with plastic
wrap when making lots
of sandwiches.

° Wrap a loaf of bread in paper towels and heat on
High for 1 to 2 minutes, until just warm.

° Avoid stringy cheese in sandwiches. Place cheese
in the center of the sandwich or add cheese during
the last 30 seconds of heating.

° Delicious treat! Toasted cheese on
a microwave browning dish or grill.
(page 124).

° Aim for thinness. Thin slices of
meat in a sandwich will heat faster
than thick slices.

° Heat taco shells on High 15 to 20 seconds before
filling.

CHICKEN OR TUNA DREAM SANDWICHES

POWER LEVEL: HIGH   SERVES: 8 sandwiches
TOTAL COOKING TIME: 1 minute per muffin
                     (2 pieces)

4 English muffins, split and toasted
1 can (6-1/2 oz.) tuna drained
             or
3/4 cup cooked chicken, finely chopped
1/2 cup mayonnaise
1/4 cup chopped celery
1/4 cup chopped onion
2 Tbsp. pickle relish
1/2 tsp. salt
8 slices green pepper or tomato
1 cup grated cheese

Place muffins on paper towel lined dish. Combine all
ingredients except pepper, tomato and cheese. Spoon
mixture over muffins and top with tomato or green pepper slices. Sprinkle cheese over sandwiches. Microwave on High 4 at a time, for 2 to 2-1/2 minutes or
until sandwiches are warm (not hot).   Repeat for
other 4 muffins.

MUFFIN PIZZAS

POWER LEVEL: HIGH   SERVES: 12 pizzas
TOTAL COOKING TIME: 1 to 1-1/2 minutes per muffin

1 Package (14 oz.) English muffins, split and toasted
1-1/2 cups pizza sauce

Pizza toppings:
    Pepperoni slices
    cooked sausage
    green pepper, chopped
    onion, chopped
    mushrooms, chopped
    mozzarella cheese, shredded

Top each muffin with 2 Tbsp. pizza sauce and a variety of toppings. Microwave 1 to 1-1/2 minutes per muffin (2 halves). Best to cook 2 muffins (4 halves) at a time on a flat dish or paper plate. Watch muffins carefully while cooking as timing can vary with the type and amount of topping.

SLOPPY JOES

POWER LEVEL: HIGH   SERVES: 6 to 8 sandwiches
TOTAL COOKING TIME: 12 to 13 minutes

1-1/2 to 2 pounds ground beef
1/2 cup onion, chopped
1/2 cup green pepper, chopped
1 can (8 oz.) tomato sauce
1/4 cup catsup
1 Tbsp. Worcestershire sauce
1/2 tsp. seasoned salt
1/8 tsp. pepper

Combine beef, onion and green pepper in a 1-1/2 quart casserole. Microwave on High for 6 to 7 minutes or until meat is browned but still pink in center. Stir twice during cooking. Drain and break up beef. Add remaining ingredients to meat mixture and cover tightly. Microwave 6 minutes on High, stirring after 3 minutes. Spoon hot sauce onto buns or Italian rolls.

NOTES _ _ _ _ _

NOW! WHAT WAS I
SUPPOSE TO REMEMBER?

38

* GROUND BEEF *

° Pay attention to defrosting ground beef - it could become a cooked meatloaf. Halfway through defrost time, break up the meat and remove soft sections already defrosted.

° Allow defrosted ground beef 5 minutes standing time to equalize the temperature and finish defrosting.

° EASY BROWNING METHOD - Brown ground beef in a plastic colander, set over a casserole or bowl. Microwave 5 to 6 minutes per pound on High, stirring and breaking up meat during cooking.

° Saute onions, celery, mushrooms or green peppers - along with browning meat.

° One hamburger can be cooked on a paper plate. Hamburgers can be cooked on a serving dish, trivet or browning dish.

° Hamburgers have the "blahs?" Make personality patties by adding grated cheese, sour cream, mushrooms, bacon, green pepper or onions. Not all together, please!

° Meatloaves have trouble cooking in the center. Microwave in a ring mold or make a hole in the middle.

° Flatten out meatloaf - don't mound it

° When meats and vegetables are cooked together, such as in a stew, cut food in similar size and shape for even cooking.

* * Note * *

An easy method to collect grease in the center of a meatloaf is to place a paper towel in the hole during cooking.

° SAVE THE BONES IN THE FREEZER! Defrost bones for stock and soup in the microwave.

° Bacon frozen stiff in the package? Heat 20 to 30 seconds on High and easily peel strips.

° MAKE 50 SLICES OF BACON TODAY AND SERVE A CROWD TO-MORROW. Microwave bacon the day before and lay it out on paper towels, cover and refrigerate. Reheat at High in the paper towels just long enough to heat well and regain crispness.

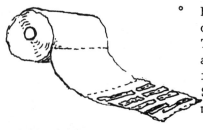

° Bacon varies in thickness of slices and quality. Timing depends on the amount of salt and sugar in the curing process. Slab bacon is not recommended for microwaving.

INTERESTING CASSEROLE TOPPINGS FOR GROUND MEAT DISHES

° Prepare 1 package (8-1/2 oz.) cornbread mix as directed on package. Five minutes before desired casserole is finished cooking, spread cornbread mix evenly in a circle on top of the dish. The center should be empty. Microwave on High, uncovered, 5 to 6 minutes or until cornbread is done.

° Spoon mounds of mashed potatoes on top of a casserole during the last 4 to 5 minutes cooking time. Sprinkle with paprika, if desired. Microwave, uncovered, on High 4 to 5 minutes.

TENDER CUTS OF MEAT

° Microwave meat thermometers are available – do not use a regular meat thermometer in a microwave oven.

** Low fat roasts like an Eye of the Round cut tend to be tough no matter how long they cook in a microwave.

° BEST TENDER MICROWAVE ROASTS ARE A ROLLED CENTER
CUT CHUCK ROAST AND A ROLLED SIRLOIN TIP ROAST.
(Round roasts cook well)

° Meats microwaved over 11 or 12 minutes will brown.
Use a browning agent (Kitchen Bouquet, Microwave
Browning Sauce, or Gravy Master) to enhance color,
if desired.

° Evenly shaped roasts cook the best. Shield bones,
roast ends and irregular edges with foil for half
the cooking time.   Hold in place with wooden toothpick.

° Turn and rotate roasts 1/2 turn halfway during
cooking.

° Don't salt meat before cooking as
it will dry out. Add other seasonings before microwaving, if
desired.

° REMEMBER THE IMPORTANCE OF CARRY-OVER COOKING WHEN
MICROWAVING MEATS. A ROAST CAN CONTINUE COOKING
15 MINUTES DURING STANDING TIME.

° DON'T TRY TO MICROWAVE A "WELL-DONE" ROAST.   RARE
AND MEDIUM MICROWAVE ROASTS ARE BEST.

  ° Serving   rare roast beef
  and a guest prefers well-
  done? Microwave selected
  slices for a minute on
  Medium on the serving
  plate.

° Place a roast on a trivet or inverted saucer to remove it from the juices.

LESS TENDER CUTS OF MEAT

° Less tender cuts of meat require lower power settings and a tight lid. Long, slow simmering aids
in tenderizing.

41

** SECRET TO TENDERIZING TOUGH MEAT

° Marinate chuck, stew meat, round steak and briskets in prepared marinade, tomato juice or wine overnight. Use commercial tenderizer, if desired.

° Steak always taste best when done in a grill or conventional broiler. Although satisfactory, steak cooked on a microwave browning dish is "SECOND BEST"

OUTDOOR COOKING WITH MICROWAVE HELP

In a hurry? Speed up outdoor barbecuing by starting the cooking in the microwave and finishing on the grill.

Precook meat and poultry 3 minutes per pound in the microwave. This method allows food such as pork chops, cornish hens, ribs and chicken to cook on the inside without burning on the outside.

Enjoy grilled steaks and hamburgers all year. Grill tender thick steaks and hamburgers on each side until seared and brown. Meat should be underdone. Cool and place meat in freezer bags or paper. When ready to use, defrost meat and place in a microwave dish. Cover lightly with wax paper. Microwave on High 3 to 4 minutes for steak and 2 to 3 minutes for hamburgers or until meat is done.

BUSY DAY LASAGNA

POWER LEVEL: HIGH AND MEDIUM   SERVES: 6
TOTAL COOKING TIME: 36 to 43 minutes

---

1 pound ground beef
3 cups meatless spaghetti sauce
1 tsp. salt
8 uncooked lasagna noodles
2 cups ricotta or cottage cheese
2 cups shredded mozzarella cheese
1/2 cup Parmesan cheese
1 Tbsp. parsley flakes
Parmesan cheese

In a 2-quart casserole, Microwave crumbled beef on High 4 to 6 minutes. Meat should be slightly pink. Drain and break up meat. Stir in spaghetti sauce and salt. Pour 1 cup sauce into a 12 x 8 inch baking dish. Place 4 uncooked noodles evenly over sauce. (They may overlap slightly) Spread half the cottage cheese over noodles. Sprinkle with 1 cup mozzarella cheese. Spoon 1 cup sauce over cheese. Repeat remaining layer with noodles, cottage cheese, mozzarella cheese and sauce. Cover tightly with plastic wrap. Microwave on High 15 minutes, rotating dish once. Then Microwave on Medium 16 to 20 minutes or until noodles are tender. Sprinkle top with Parmesan cheese and Microwave, uncovered, on High 1 to 2 minutes until cheese melts. Let stand 10 minutes before serving.

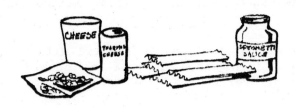

STUFFED FLANK STEAK

POWER LEVEL: MEDIUM   SERVES: 4 to 6
TOTAL COOKING TIME: 20 to 23 minutes

1-1/2 to 2 pound flank steak
1 cup marinade
Stuffing variation

Pound flank steak with a mallet or dish side to flatten and tenderize. Marinate meat overnight in 1 cup
French dressing, tomato juice or a prepared marinade.
Spread stuffing over meat, leaving 1 inch border on
all sides. Roll up jelly roll style and secure with
string in three places. Place seam side up in low
baking dish. Top with marinade and cover tightly with
plastic wrap. Microwave on Medium for 20 to 23 minutes
until fork tender. After 10 minutes cooking time, turn
meat seam side down and baste with marinade. Let stand
5 minutes before serving.

STUFFING VARIATIONS:

SAUSAGE STUFFING: Brown 1/2 pound bulk pork sausage.
Drain and mix together 1/4 cup chopped celery, 1/2 cup
crushed crackers, 1/2 cup chopped apple and 1 Tbsp.
minced dry onion.

VEGETABLE STUFFING: Combine 1/2 cup seasoned bread
crumbs, 1/4 cup chopped celery, 2 Tbsp. chopped onion,
1/4 cup chopped mushrooms, 1 Tbsp. Parmesan cheese,
1/2 tsp. seasoned salt and 1 Tbsp. melted butter or
margarine.

NOTE: Each end of meat may be covered with a strip of
       foil 1 inch wide for half of cooking time to
       prevent overcooking.

THE ALL AMERICAN HOT DOG

POWER LEVEL: HIGH
TOTAL COOKING TIME: 25 to 30 seconds per wiener

Wieners are precooked and only need to be heated. Score or prick the top of each wiener to prevent curling or splitting. When microwaving wieners, place on a napkin, paper plate or any microwave-safe plate. Microwave each wiener on High for 25 to 30 seconds. If cooking the hot dog in the bun, wrap in a paper towel or paper napkin to help absorb moisture. Buns and hot dogs heated together have a slightly soggy texture. Children enjoy cooking hot dogs in the bun and don't seem to notice.

Be creative with a simple hot dog! Wieners can be wrapped in a slice of partially cooked bacon, topped with a slice of cheese or covered with tomato sauce, Italian herbs, and mozzarella cheese for Pizza-dogs.

WIENERS AND SAUERKRAUT

POWER LEVEL: HIGH   SERVES: 4
TOTAL COOKING TIME: 7 to 9 minutes

8 wieners, cut in half
1 can (12 oz.) light beer or ginger ale
1 medium apple, chopped
1 can (16 oz.) sauerkraut, drained
1 tsp. cornstarch
2-1/2 tsp. caraway seeds

Combine all ingredients in a 1-1/2 to 2-quart casserole. Push wieners to bottom of dish. Cover. Microwave on High 7 to 9 minutes until hot, stirring after 5 minutes.

45

POWER LEVEL: MEDIUM   SERVES: 4 to 6
TOTAL COOKING TIME: 13 to 15 minutes per pound or
                        TEMPERATURE PROBE at 170°

1 pork roast (3 to 5 pounds)   2 tsp. browning agent

Shield ends of bone-in roast with small pieces of foil, or tie boned roast compactly. Brush roast with browning agent. Place roast, fat side down, on a rack or trivet in a 12 x 8 inch baking dish. Cover with waxed paper. Microwave on Medium for 13 to 15 minutes per pound. Half-way through cooking time, remove foil sheilds and turn roast fat side up. When finished, remove roast to platter and cover with foil tent. Let stand 20 minutes. Glaze of your choice may be spooned over roast during last half of cooking time.

GLAZE VARIATIONS:

APPLE GLAZE - Mix together 1 cup apple pie filling, 1/4 cup raisins and 1/2 tsp. of cinnamon. Spread on pork roast or ham.

APRICOT GLAZE - Mix together 1 cup apricot preserves, 1/4 cup orange juice, 1 Tbsp. lemon juice and 1/2 tsp. ginger. Microwave on High for 3 minutes. Spread on pork roast or ham.

SHERRIED CURRANT GLAZE - Mix together 1 (10 oz.) jar currant jelly, 2 Tbsp. dry sherry and 1 Tbsp. soy sauce. Microwave on High for 3 minutes. Spread on pork roast or ham.

SPICY GLAZED SPARERIBS

POWER LEVEL: HIGH   SERVES: 4
TOTAL COOKING TIME: 30 to 38 minutes

3/4 tsp. liquid smoke
1 tsp. garlic salt
1/4 tsp. pepper
1 tsp. cinnamon
1/4 cup brown sugar
1/4 cup soy sauce
1 cup orange juice
1-1/2 Tbsp. cornstarch
2 Tbsp. water
2-1/2 to 3 pounds spareribs, rack or riblets

Mix all ingredients except ribs, cornstarch and water
to make marinade. Brush ribs with marinade. Place
ribs in a 12 x 8 or 13 x 9 inch dish, bone side up.
Cover with waxed paper. Microwave on High for 15 to
20 minutes. Drain and turn meat over. Add remaining
marinade. Cover with waxed paper and Microwave 15 to
18 minutes on High until meat is no longer pink.
Drain off marinade. Pour excess fat from top of marinade. Add cornstarch and water to marinade. Microwave on High 2 to 3 minutes, stirring every minute
until sauce is clear and thick. Spoon over spareribs.

VARIATIONS:

TENDER BARBECUED SPARERIBS: Add 2 cups water to spareribs and cover tightly. Microwave at Medium for 65 to
70 minutes. Drain and add 1 cup barbecue sauce. Cover
tightly and Microwave on Medium for 10 to 15 minutes.
Spoon barbecue sauce over ribs.

JIFFY PORK CHOP CASSEROLE

POWER LEVEL: MEDIUM HIGH   SERVES: 4
TOTAL COOKING TIME: 18 to 22 minutes

4 pork chops, 1/2 inch thick
1 tsp. dried parsley (optional)
1/2 tsp. salt
1 can (3 oz.) French fried onion rings, divided
1 can (10-1/2 oz.) golden mushroom soup

Arrange pork chops with meatiest portion to the outside of casserole. Sprinkle with parsley and salt.
Arrange half of onion rings over chops and spoon mushroom soup on top. Cover tightly and Microwave on
Medium High for 18 to 22 minutes. Top with remaining
onion rings. Let stand 3 minutes, covered.

NOTE: I like to use a browning dish for this recipe.
       Although it is not neccessary to brown chops,
       I believe it enhances flavor.

HAM TETRAZZINI - ONE POT MEAL

POWER LEVEL: HIGH   SERVES: 6
TOTAL COOKING TIME: 18 to 20 minutes

1 cup uncooked spaghetti, broken into 1 inch pieces
2 cups cooked ham, cubed
1 can (10-3/4 oz.) cream of chicken soup
3/4 cup milk
1 box (10 oz.) frozen mixed vegetables, slightly
  thawed
1 can (3 oz.) sliced mushrooms, drained
1/2 tsp. salt
1 cup shredded Cheddar cheese

48

Combine all ingredients except cheese in a 2-1/2 quart casserole. Stir well. Cover tightly and Microwave on High 18 to 20 minutes. Stir twice during cooking. Sprinkle with cheese and let stand, covered, 5 minutes until cheese melts.

JOHNNY MAZETTE-ONE POT MEAL

TOTAL LEVEL: HIGH AND MEDIUM   SERVES: 6
TOTAL COOKING TIME: 30 to 34 minutes

1 pound ground beef
1/4 cup green pepper, chopped
1/2 cup onion, chopped
1 Tbsp. chili powder (optional)
1 tsp. garlic salt
1 package (8 oz.) fine egg noodles
1 can (10-3/4 oz.) condensed tomato soup
1 can (10-3/4 oz.) condensed mushroom soup
1 cup water
1 cup shredded Cheddar cheese or diced American
   process cheese

Place crumbled ground beef, green pepper and onion in a 3-quart casserole. Microwave 4 to 6 minutes on High. Drain off fat and break up ground beef. Sprinkle chili powder, salt and noodles over top. Mix soups and water together. Pour over meat and noodles. Cover tightly. Microwave 10 minutes on High. Stir well, making sure all noodles are covered with liquid. Microwave on Medium for 16 to 18 minutes or until noodles are soft. Sprinkle with cheese and let stand, covered, 5 minutes.

CHILI

POWER LEVEL: HIGH   SERVES: 4 to 6
TOTAL COOKING TIME: 14 to 18 minutes

1 pound ground beef
1 medium onion, chopped
1 medium green pepper, chopped
1 can (1 lb.) tomatoes, undrained
1 can (8 oz.) tomato sauce
1/3 cup catsup
1 can (1 lb.) kidney beans, drained
1 to 2 tsp. chili powder
1/4 tsp. garlic salt
1 tsp. salt
1 bay leaf

Place crumbled beef, onion and green pepper in a 2-quart casserole. Microwave on High 4 to 6 minutes. Drain off fat and break up ground beef. Stir in remaining ingredients. Microwave 10 to 12 minutes on High, covered tightly. Stir twice during cooking. Let stand 5 minutes. Remove bay leaf before serving. Sprinkle with grated cheese for tasty topping.

DELICIOUS POT ROAST

POWER LEVEL: MEDIUM   SERVES: 6
TOTAL COOKING TIME: 1 hour to 1 hour 15 minutes

1 package dry onion soup mix
1 can (12 oz.) beer or 1 can (12 oz.) gingerale
1/2 tsp. garlic salt
1/4 tsp. pepper
2 to 3 pound pot roast
3 small potatoes, quartered
3 carrots, cut in 1/2 slices
3 stalks celery, cut in 1 inch pieces

Place meat in a large size (14 x 20) plastic roasting bag in a baking dish.

Combine onion soup mix, beer or gingerale, salt and pepper in bag. Turn bag gently to mix. Close bag with string or rubber band. Marinate overnight. Turn roast once.

When ready to cook, make 3 or 4 small slits in the top of bag for steam to escape. Microwave on Medium for 1 hour to 1 hour and 15 minutes. Halfway through cooking, turn meat and add vegetables to bag.

BASIC BEEF STEW

POWER LEVEL: MEDIUM AND MEDIUM HIGH   SERVES: 6
TOTAL COOKING TIME: 115 to 125 minutes

---

2 pounds beef stew meat, cut in 1/2 inch pieces
2 cups water
2 cans (6 oz.) tomato paste
1 Tbsp. instant beef bouillon
1 bay leaf
1 tsp. salt
1/8 tsp. pepper
2 medium potatoes, cut in 1 inch cubes
2 medium carrots, cut into 1/4 inch pieces
2 celery stalks, cut into 1/2 inch pieces
1 can (12 oz.) yellow kernel corn, drained

In a 3-quart casserole, combine meat, water, tomato paste, bouillon, bay leaf, salt and pepper. Stir well. If desired, marinate 3 to 4 hours or overnight to make meat more tender. Cover casserole tightly and Microwave on Medium for 1 hour 30 minutes. Stir twice during cooking. Add vegetables and cover again. Microwave at Medium High for 25 to 35 more minutes. Let stand 5 to 10 minutes before serving.

HAM LOAF

POWER SETTING: MEDIUM HIGH   SERVES: 4 to 6
TOTAL COOKING TIME: 20 to 22 minutes
                        TEMPERATURE PROBE - 170°

1 pound ground cooked ham
1/2 pound ground pork
3/4 cup soft bread crumbs
1/4 cup milk
2 eggs
1/4 cup chopped onion
1 tsp. brown sugar
1/4 tsp. cinnamon
1/8 tsp. pepper

Mix together all ingredients and stir until well blended. Shape into flat oval loaf in a 10 x 6 baking dish
or a 9-inch pie pan. Cover tightly and Microwave at
Medium High for 20 to 22 minutes or until set. Let
stand 5 minutes. Ham Loaf can be topped with fruit
preserves, horseradish sauce or brown sugar before
serving.

SWISS STEAK

POWER LEVEL: MEDIUM   SERVES: 4 to 6
TOTAL COOKING TIME: 70 to 80 minutes

1-1/2 to 2 pounds beef round steak, cut in 1/2 inch
                              serving pieces
1 can (8 oz.) tomato sauce
1/2 cup red wine or water
1 pkg. dry onion soup mix
1 tsp. Worcestershire sauce
1/4 cup flour
1/4 tsp. salt
1/8 tsp. pepper
1 onion, sliced

Pound swiss steak with a mallet or dish side to tenderize. Refrigerate meat overnight in a 12 x 8 inch dish covered with a mixture of tomato sauce, wine or water, onion soup mix and Worcestershire sauce. Drain and save marinade. Dredge meat in coating of flour, salt and pepper. Arrange meat in dish and add onion. Top with tomato sauce marinade and cover tightly. Microwave on Medium 70 to 80 minutes, rearranging meat after 35 minutes, until tender.

STUFFED GREEN PEPPERS

POWER LEVEL: MEDIUM HIGH   SERVES: 4
TOTAL COOKING TIME: 15 to 18 minutes

---

1 pound ground beef
1-1/4 cup uncooked instant rice
1 egg, beaten
1 small onion, chopped
1 can (8 oz.) tomato sauce
1 tsp. Italian seasonings (optional)
1/2 tsp. salt
1/4 tsp. pepper
4 large green peppers

Remove tops, membrane and seeds from peppers. Mix together all ingredients except peppers. Stuff peppers with mixture. Place peppers in a 8 or 9-inch baking dish and cover tightly with lid or plastic wrap. Microwave on Medium High for 15 to 18 minutes or until meat is no longer pink and rice is soft. Let stand 5 minutes before serving.

NOTE: Pour 1 cup tomato sauce or 1 can tomato soup over peppers before microwaving for "saucier" peppers.

NOTES_____

ANOTHER PAGE
FOR ME !!

* POULTRY *

° "Loud popping noises scare me. Am I a chicken?" No, you are not. It's the chicken in the oven that needs its skin pierced before cooking to allow steam to escape.

° Poultry looks anemic and usually needs added color. Try barbecue sauce, paprika and butter, soy sauce or a jelly glaze to give a lively appearance.

° Direct salting of poultry will draw moisture to the surface and cause the bird to dry out. A non-salted vegetable oil or drippings are best for basting.

° Defrost all poultry completely and rotate frozen meats and poultry during defrosting.

° Need chicken for a salad or casserole? Add 1/2 cup water to plain chicken and steam it, covered tightly, for 6 minutes per pound on High.

° "I want fried chicken like Mama used to make." Try the recipe on page 60. The taste and appearance is almost the same as conventional fried chicken. DO NOT fry chicken in a large amount of fat, like Mama did, it can become dangerously hot in the microwave oven.

° Cover poultry lightly with wax paper to prevent spattering.

° Whole chickens and turkeys up to 12 pounds can be successfully microwaved. A turkey over 12 pounds will cook more evenly in a conventional oven.

° A roasted bird should be well trussed. Shield wings and ends of legs with small pieces of foil for half the cooking time.

- Stuff a bird loosely and add 4 to 5 minutes per pound of <u>stuffing</u> to the cooking time.

- Rotate the bird halfway during cooking for evenness.

- Don't count on a poultry plastic pop-up indicator. They either register too late or may melt. Remove for microwaving.

- "My chicken is in the bag and falling apart" Foods done in a cooking bag maintain flavor, moisture and vitamins but have shorter cooking times. A plastic bag is a great way to get tenderness but "overcook" and you have chicken stew.

- The secret of evenly cooked chicken pieces is to rotate and rearrange the chicken 2 or 3 times during microwaving. This may be more often than the recipe calls for and can be boring but it produces perfect chicken.

- ECONOMY COATING: A use for leftover, unsweetened cereal the children haven't eaten. One cup of any crushed cereal with 3/4 tsp. garlic salt added makes delicious chicken coating.

STUFFED CORNISH HENS

POWER LEVEL: MEDIUM HIGH   SERVES: 4
TOTAL COOKING TIME: 40 to 42 minutes

---

4 Cornish Hens, 1 pound each
4 cups stuffing, bread or rice
2 Tbsp. browning agent mixed with 2 Tbsp. melted butter

Stuff hens and brush with browning mixture. Place hens breast side down and at least 1 inch apart in a flat dish. Cover with waxed paper. Microwave on Medium High for 40 to 42 minutes. Turn hens breast side up halfway through cooking time. Baste with browning agent periodically during cooking.

56

VARIATION:

CRANBERRRY-ORANGE CORNISH HENS - Brush 2 Cornish Hens, split (4 halves) with a mixture of 1 tsp. browning agent and 1 Tbsp. honey. Cover with waxed paper. Microwave, skin side down, on High for 8 minutes. Turn halves over and baste with browning agent. Top with 1/2 of a 16 oz. can of whole cranberry sauce. Cover again and Microwave on High 8 minutes. Top with remaining cranberry sauce and sprinkle with 1 Tbsp. dried orange peel. Microwave, uncovered, on High 3 to 5 minutes or until done.

CHICKEN A LA KING

POWER LEVEL: HIGH AND MEDIUM HIGH   SERVES: 4 to 6
TOTAL COOKING TIME: 17 to 21 minutes

1/2 cup butter or margarine
1/2 cup unsifted all-purpose flour
2 cups milk
1 cup chicken broth
2 to 3 cups cubed, cooked chicken
1 can (4 oz.) mushroom stems and pieces, undrained
1/2 cup diced green pepper
2 Tbsp. chopped pimento
1 tsp. salt
1/4 tsp. pepper

In 2-quart casserole place butter. Microwave on High for 1 minute until melted. Blend in flour. Gradually stir in milk and broth. Mix well. Microwave on High for 8 to 10 minutes, stirring with a rotary beater or whisk after 4 minutes. Sauce should be thick and smooth. Mix in chicken, mushrooms, pepper, pimento, salt and pepper. Cover tightly, and Microwave at Medium High for 8 to 10 minutes. Stir twice during cooking. Let stand 5 to 10 minutes.

ITALIAN CHICKEN

POWER LEVEL: HIGH   SERVES: 4 to 6
TOTAL COOKING TIME: 20 to 24 minutes

2-1/2 to 3-1/2 pounds chicken pieces
2 medium onions, thinly sliced
2 small green peppers, cut in strips
1 can (10 oz.) condensed tomato soup
1 can (6 oz.) tomato paste
1/4 cup red wine (optional)
1/2 tsp. oregano
1/2 tsp. garlic salt
1/4 tsp. thyme
1 cup (4 oz.) shredded Mozzarella cheese

Remove skin from chicken pieces and arrange in 12 x 9
inch baking dish, thicker parts near the edge of dish.
Arrange onion and pepper slices around the chicken.
In mixing bowl stir together soup, tomato paste, wine
and seasonings. Spoon sauce over chicken. Cover with
waxed paper and Microwave on High for 20 to 24 minutes.
Rotate dish 1/2 turn after 10 minutes. Sprinkle with
cheese and let stand, covered with waxed paper, for 5
minutes.

CHICKEN AND DUMPLINGS

POWER LEVEL: HIGH   SERVES: 4 to 6
TOTAL COOKING TIME: 32 to 40 minutes

2-1/2 to 3 pounds chicken, cut in pieces
2 medium onions, quartered
3 carrots, cut in 1/2 inch pieces
4 parsley springs   2 bay leaves
1 can (13 3/4 oz.) chicken broth   1/4 tsp thyme
2 cups water   Dash of pepper
2 tsp. salt   1/3 cup water
1/4 tsp poultry seasoning   3 Tbsp. cornstar

58

DUMPLINGS

1 cup biscuit baking mix
1/3 cup milk
1/4 tsp. poultry seasoning

Place chicken, vegetables, parsley, broth, water and seasonings in a 4 quart casserole. Microwave, covered tightly, on High 25 to 30 minutes or until vegetables are tender. Remove chicken and add mixture of cornstarch and 1/3 cup water to casserole. Microwave on High 3 to 4 minutes until mixture thickens. Return chicken to casserole. Mix together dumpling ingredients until moistened. Spoon mixture over casserole. Microwave, covered, on High 4 to 6 minutes or until dumplings are done.

CHEESE - TACO DRUMSTICKS

POWER LEVEL: HIGH   SERVES: 8 Drumsticks
TOTAL COOKING TIME: 10 to 11 minutes

---

8 chicken drumsticks, skin removed
1/4 cup butter or margarine, melted
1 cup crushed Cheddar cheese crackers
1-1/2 Tbsp. taco seasoning mix

Dip each drumstick in melted butter and coat with a mixture of crackers and taco seasoning mix. Arrange drumsticks on roasting rack or in a 12 x 8 inch baking dish. Place meatiest portion to outside of pan. Cover with waxed paper. Microwave on High 5 minutes. Turn each drumstick over, cover again and Microwave 5 to 6 minutes more, until meat is no longer pink. Let stand 3 minutes before serving.

NOTE: Dip drumsticks into taco sauce when serving if desired.

OVEN FRIED CHICKEN

POWER LEVEL: HIGH   SERVES: 4 to 6
TOTAL COOKING TIME: 20 to 24 minutes

1/3 cup butter or margarine, melted
1 cup corn flake crumbs
1/2 tsp. poultry seasoning
1 tsp. salt
2-1/2 to 3-1/2 pounds cut up frying chicken (skin removed)

Melt butter in a 12 x 8 inch shallow baking dish. Combine crumbs, poultry seasoning and salt on plate or in a bag. Roll chicken pieces in melted butter and coat with crumb mixture. Return chicken to 12 x 8 inch dish, placing meatiest pieces to the outside of dish. Microwave on High 20 to 24 minutes or until fork tender. Turn and rearrange chicken after 10 minutes.

VARIATIONS:

STUFFING COATED CHICKEN: Follow directions for Oven Fried Chicken but substitute 1 cup finely crushed package stuffing mix or herb seasoned croutons for coating.

CHICKEN PARMESAN: Follow directions for Oven Fried Chicken but substitute 1 cup bread crumbs and 1/4 Parmesan cheese for coating.

ONION TOPPER CHICKEN: Follow directions for Oven Fried Chicken but substitute 1 package dried onion soup mix for coating.

SHAKE AND BAKE CHICKEN: Follow directions for Oven Fried Chicken but substitute 1 package commercially prepared coating mix for coating.

ONE-POT CHICKEN AND RICE

POWER LEVEL: HIGH AND MEDIUM   SERVES: 6
TOTAL COOKING TIME: 40 to 45 minutes

---

1 cup uncooked long grain rice
1 tsp. salt
1 small onion, sliced
1 can (10 oz.) condensed golden mushroom soup
1 cup water or chicken broth
2 to 3 pounds chicken pieces

Combine all ingredients except chicken in 3-quart casserole. Place chicken over top of mixture. Cover tightly with larger pieces to the outer edge of the dish. Microwave on High for 15 minutes. Rearrange chicken and stir rice lightly.

Cover tightly and Microwave on Medium for 25 to 30 minutes or until rice and chicken are done. Let stand, covered, 5 minutes before serving.

NOTE: Brush chicken before cooking with 1 Tbsp. browning agent diluted with 1 Tbsp. water, for added color.

VARIATION: Substitute 4 or 5 Pork Chops in place of chicken.

CHICKEN TERIYAKI

POWER LEVEL: HIGH   SERVES: 4
TOTAL COOKING TIME: 22 to 24 minutes

1/2 cup soy sauce
2 Tbsp. brown sugar
1/4 cup sherry wine
1 clove garlic, minced
1/2 tsp. ground ginger
3 pounds chicken, cut up

In a 12 x 9 baking dish, mix all ingredients except chicken. Heat for 1 minute on High to dissolve sugar. Add chicken and coat with sauce. Marinate several hours or overnight in the refrigerator.

Cover dish with waxed paper. Microwave on High for 22 to 24 minutes or until tender. Turn the chicken over and brush with drippings halfway through cooking. Let stand 5 minutes.

QUICK CHICKEN WITH SOUP

POWER LEVEL: HIGH   SERVES: 4
TOTAL COOKING TIME: 18 to 22 minutes

2-1/2 to 3-1/2 pounds chicken pieces
1/2 tsp. salt
1 can (10 oz.) condensed soup

Place chicken skin side up in a 12 x 8 inch dish with the thickest pieces to the edge of the dish. Spread soup and salt over chicken. Cover with waxed paper. Microwave on High 18 to 22 minutes. Rotate dish 1/2 turns after 10 minutes. Let stand 5 minutes before serving.

Chicken Curry

Add 1 tsp. curry powder to 1 can condensed Cream of Chicken Soup. Sprinkle 1/4 cup chopped nuts over chicken before serving.

Mexican Chicken

Add 2 Tbsp. diced green chilies, 1 tsp. instant minced onion, and 2 Tbsp. taco seasoning mix to condensed Cheddar cheese soup.

* FISH AND SEAFOOD *

° DELICIOUS, DELICIOUS is seafood cooked in a micro-wave. Five star rating for sure!

° Remember seafood is delicate and can be quickly overcooked. Follow the minimum time suggested, let the fish stand a few minutes and then test for doneness.

° Avoid serving tough Trout. Micro-wave fish until the outer edges appear opaque but the center is still slightly trans-lucent. Cover during standing time to help the center cook completely.

° If a fish is "flaky", it's done.

° <u>Start fishing early in the day.</u> When preparing fish ahead to serve later, undercook slightly and reheat on High to desired doneness just before serving time.

° To steam fish - don't add water. Cover the dish with a moistened paper towel.

° "It's so hard to look a cooking fish in the eye." When micro-waving a whole fish, cover the head and tail with foil to prevent overcooking and avoid that "fishy stare".

° Prick the skin of a whole fish. They can fill with steam and blow up. Serve blown-up fish on cracker for appetizers.

° A browning dish is super for grilling fish.

° Fish is usually cooked 4 to 6 minutes per pound on High.

- "My fish was so wet, I thought it would swim off the dinner table." Next time, dry the fish thoroughly and line the dish with a paper towel during cooking to absorb excess juices.

- Keep thicker edges and larger fish pieces toward the outside of the cooking dish.

- Cooking time is the same whether seafood is in or out of it's shell.

- Arrange shrimp and scallops in a circle when microwaving.

- WARM UP A COLD FISH. Defrost frozen fish for a minimum time until the pieces just begin to separate. Let the fish stand until completely thawed or hold it under cold running water.

- When defrosting a package of frozen fish, place small pieces of foil over the ends of the box so the fish thaws evenly.

- Frozen fish that has been thawed will take a little longer to microwave than fresh fish.

STEAMED FISH

POWER LEVEL: HIGH   SERVES: 4
TOTAL COOKING TIME: 5 to 7 minutes

---

1 pound fish fillets, fresh or defrosted
2 Tbsp. butter or margarine, melted
2 Tbsp. white wine or 1 Tbsp. lemon juice
1/2 tsp. salt
Dash of pepper
1/4 tsp. dill weed (optional)
Paprika

In a 12 x 8 inch dish, arrange fillets with thickest pieces toward the outside of the dish. Add melted butter, wine or lemon juice, salt, pepper and dill weed to top of fish. Sprinkle with paprika. Cover tightly with plastic wrap or lid. Microwave on High 5 to 7 minutes or until fish flakes with a fork. Rotate dish 1/2 turn after 3 minutes. Let fish stand 3 to 5 minutes before serving.

STUFFED FISH ROLL-UPS

POWER LEVEL: HIGH   SERVES: 4
TOTAL COOKING TIME: 5 to 7 minutes

---

4 fish fillets, fresh or defrosted
1/4 cup carrots, finely grated
1/4 cup green onions, finely chopped
1/4 cup green pepper, finely chopped
1/4 cup fine dry bread crumbs
1 egg, ·beaten
1/2 tsp. salt
1 tsp. parsley flakes
1 Tbsp. butter or margarine, melted
Paprika
1/2 cup Thousand Island, French or Creamy Italian dressing, warmed

Combine carrots, onions, pepper, crumbs, egg, salt and parsley flakes. Spoon mixture on top of each fillet. Roll up fillets and secure with one or two toothpicks. Place in 8 or 9 inch dish. Brush with melted butter and sprinkle with paprika. Cover with waxed paper and Microwave on High 5 to 7 minutes, or until fish flakes easily. Rotate dish once during cooking. Remove toothpicks and top with dressing. Let stand, uncovered, 3 minutes.

HERB COATED FISH FILLETS

POWER LEVEL: HIGH   SERVES: 4
TOTAL COOKING TIME: 4 to 5 min/per lb.

---

4 fish fillets, fresh or defrosted
1/2 cup crushed cornflakes
1/2 cup grated Parmesan cheese
1/3 cup minced fresh parsley
1/2 tsp. garlic powder
1/4 tsp. salt
1 egg, beaten

Rinse and dry fillets. Mix remaining dry ingredients
in a pie plate. Dip fillets in egg and crumb mixture
to coat. Arrange in 12 x 8 inch baking dish and cover
with paper towel. Microwave on High for 4 to 5 minutes per pound.

SALMON OR TUNA LOAF

POWER LEVEL: HIGH   SERVES: 4 to 6
TOTAL COOKING TIME: 8 to 10 minutes

---

1 can (1 lb.) salmon or 2 cans (6-1/2 oz.) tuna,
drained
2 eggs
1/2 cup bread crumbs
1/2 cup milk
1/4 cup onions, chopped
1/4 cup celery, chopped
1 tsp. lemon juice
1 tsp. dried parsley
1/4 tsp. salt
Paprika

Mix all ingredients together except paprika. Place mixture in a 1-1/2 quart ring mold or casserole. Sprinkle with paprika. Microwave on High for 8 to 10 minutes. Turn dish 1/2 turn halfway through cooking. Allow 5 minutes standing time before serving. Top with Cucumber Sauce, if desired.

CUCUMBER SAUCE: Combine 1/2 cup sour cream, 1/2 cup chopped cucumber, 2 green onions, chopped and 2 Tbsp. milk. Microwave 1 minute on Medium to warm.

SCALLOPED FISH

POWER LEVEL: HIGH   SERVES: 4
TOTAL COOKING TIME: 7 to 10 minutes

1/4 cup butter or margarine
1 cup saltine cracker crumbs
1/2 tsp. salt
Dash pepper
1 Tbsp. dried parsley flakes
1 pound white fish fillet, fresh or thawed
1/2 cup milk or cream
Paprika

Melt butter on High 1 minute in a 1-quart measure. Add cracker crumbs, salt, pepper and parsley. Mix well. Place fish on a 9 or 10 inch pie plate with thickest ends toward outer dish. Cover with waxed paper and Microwave on High 3 to 4 minutes. Sprinkle fish with crumb mixture and paprika. Pour milk or cream evenly over top. Microwave, uncovered, on High 3 to 5 minutes until fish flakes easily with fork. Let stand 5 minutes before serving.

CREAMED TUNA

POWER LEVEL: HIGH AND MEDIUM HIGH   SERVES: 4 to 6
TOTAL COOKING TIME: 11 to 13 minutes

2 Tbsp. butter   1 cup milk
1/4 cup onion, chopped   1 Tbsp. lemon juice
1/4 cup green pepper, chopped
1 can (10-3/4 oz.) condensed cream of shrimp soup
1 can (4 oz.) mushrooms, drained
2 cans (6-1/2 oz.) tuna, drained and flaked

In a 2-quart casserole, place butter, onion and green pepper. Microwave 2 minutes on High. Add soup, mushrooms, milk, lemon juice and tuna to casserole. Cover tightly and Microwave on Medium High 9 to 11 minutes until heated. Stir halfway through cooking. Serve over rice, noodles, toast or patty shells.

VARIATION: Substitute 1 small can shrimp, crabmeat or diced lobster for tuna.

ORIENTAL TUNA CASSEROLE

POWER LEVEL: MEDIUM HIGH   SERVES: 4
TOTAL COOKING TIME: 11 to 13 minutes

1 can (3 oz.) chow mein noodles
1 can (6-1/2 oz.) tuna, drained
1 can (10-3/4 oz.) cream of mushroom soup
1/4 cup milk
1 box (10 oz.) frozen oriental vegetables, slightly thawed
1 Tbsp. soy sauce

Reserve 1/2 can chow mein noodles. Combine all remaining ingredients in a 2-quart casserole. Microwave on Medium High 11 to 13 minutes until hot. Stir once during cooking. Sprinkle with remaining noodles on top. Let stand 3 to 5 minutes.

* EGGS *

o NEVER MICROWAVE AN EGG IN THE SHELL. Boom!

o Remember that eggs are delicate and should be slightly undercooked. Beginners have been known to overcook eggs until they turn green and couldn't be cut with a saw.

o Scrambled eggs are easy and are one of the best microwave products. Try them at once, if you haven't already.

o Add water instead of milk to scrambled eggs for fluffiness. A little butter or margarine added prevents sticking.

o Start scrambled eggs in a large enough container. They expand greatly. Stir frequently.

o Cheesy eggs. Add cheese to scrambled eggs after cooking and stir until melted.

o Use a lower power (Medium) for poached, baked and shirred eggs. This gives the egg white time to catch up with the fast-cooking yolk.

o Easy hard-cooked eggs. Break 6 eggs into a pie plate or 6 oz. custard cups. Gently pierce yolks and cover tightly with plastic wrap. Microwave on Medium for 6 minutes or until yolk is soft and white is opaque. (may take longer for large eggs) Rotate dishes 1/2 turn once during cooking. Let stand, covered, 3 to 4 minutes. Cool completely and dice.

WHOOPS!

SPANISH SCRAMBLED EGGS

POWER LEVEL: HIGH   SERVES: 2 to 3
TOTAL COOKING TIME: 5 to 7 minutes

1/2 cup chopped green pepper
1 Tbsp. butter or margarine
6 eggs, beaten
3 Tbsp. milk
1/2 tsp. salt
1/4 tsp. pepper

1/2 tsp. oregano
1/3 cup tomatoes
   chopped
1/2 cup shredded
   mozzarella cheese

Place green pepper and butter in 1-quart casserole or
10 inch pie plate. Microwave on High 1 to 2 minutes.
Blend eggs, milk, salt, pepper and oregano in a small
bowl. Add to green pepper and butter. Mix well. Microwave on High for 4 to 5 minutes or until egg mixture is
set. Stir for 30 seconds. Blend in tomatoes and cheese.
Allow 3 minutes standing time.

COTTAGE SCRAMBLED EGGS

POWER LEVEL: HIGH   SERVES: 4
TOTAL COOKING TIME: 5 to 7 minutes

1 Tbsp. butter or margarine
2 Tbsp. onion, chopped
4 to 5 eggs
3/4 cup bacon or ham, crumbled
1/4 cup fresh or canned mushrooms
1/4 cup creamed cottage cheese
Paprika

In a 9 or 10 inch pie plate place butter and onions.
Microwave on High 1 to 2 minutes. Add eggs to onion
mixture and beat thoroughly. Add meat and mushrooms.
Microwave on High 4 to 5 minutes. Stir twice during
cooking. Stir in cottage cheese until slightly melted.
Do not overstir.

70

* CHEESE *

° Slice cheese easily. Heat cold cheese 1/2 second to 1 minute on Medium.

° Soften cream cheese for dips and spreads. Remove foil and Microwave on Medium for 1 to 1-1/2 minutes.

° Appetizer and process cheese spreads can be softened and made more spreadable. Remove the metal lid and heat the jar for no longer than 15 to 20 seconds on High.

° TAKE CARE! Cheese melts quickly, due to high fat content. It will become hard and stringy when over-cooked. Heat natural cheese products on Medium.

° The cheese topping on a microwave recipe should be added after cooking. Heat from the food will melt the cheese. One or 2 minutes added time may be needed for thick cheese topping.

° EASY CHEESE TOPPING

Place 1 jar or package (8 oz.) processed cheese food in a small bowl. Microwave on Medium High 3 minutes or until cheese is melted. Stir until smooth. For thinner sauce, add a Tbsp. milk, beer or tomato juice.

° Shred or cube cheese in a recipe for quick micro-wave cooking.

° American favorite. Place a slice of cheese on a piece of pie and heat for 15 seconds.

° Life and cooking are made easier with condensed Cheddar cheese soup.

° To make vegetable cheese sauce, place a 10 oz. can of condensed cheddar cheese soup, diluted with 1/2 milk, in the microwave oven on High for 2 to 3 minutes. Stir and pour.

° Old, ratty-looking cheese can become a revitalized sauce. Add 1/4 cup finely grated cheese to 1 cup of hot basic white sauce. Heat on Medium power for 2 to 4 minutes. Let stand for a few minutes until cheese melts.

° EASY CHEESY FONDUE

Combine 1 can (10 oz.) condensed cream of shrimp soup and 1 roll (6 oz.) process garlic or onion flavored cheese, cubed. Microwave on High for 3 to 4 minutes, stirring once. Tastes like a Gourmet treat! Serves 2 to 3 but can be doubled or tripled for a party.

CHEESE SANDWICH CASSEROLE

POWER LEVEL: MEDIUM   SERVES: 2
TOTAL COOKING TIME: 9 to 12 minutes

---

4 slices bread
Butter or margarine
2 cups (8 oz.) shredded Cheddar cheese
2 eggs
1 cup dairy half and half
2 Tbsp. butter or margarine, melted
1/4 tsp. salt
1/2 tsp. dry mustard
1/4 tsp. paprika

Spread each slice of bread with butter. In a 10 x 6 x 2 inch dish place 2 slices bread, butter side up. Top with 1 cup shredded cheese. Repeat layers. In mixing bowl, beat eggs. Blend in cream, butter, salt, mustard and paprika. Pour mixture over sandwiches. Cover with waxed paper and Microwave on Medium 9 to 12 minutes. Rotate dish 1/4 turn every 3 minutes. Let stand 5 minutes before serving.

72

MACARONI AND CHEESE

POWER LEVEL: HIGH AND MEDIUM HIGH   SERVES: 6
TOTAL COOKING TIME: 23 to 29 minutes

---

1 package (7 or 8 oz.) macaroni
3 cups very hot water
2 tsp. salt
3 Tbsp. butter or margarine
3 Tbsp. flour
1/2 tsp. salt

Dash of pepper
2 cups milk
2 cups shredded
   sharp cheese

In a 2-quart casserole, combine macaroni, water and
salt. Cover tightly and microwave on high for 10 to
12 minutes. Stir after 5 minutes. Drain well. In
another 2-quart casserole, Microwave butter for 1 minute on High. Add flour, salt and pepper. Gradually
add milk, stirring until smooth. Microwave on High
for 6 to 8 minutes until thickened. Stir frequently
to prevent lumping. Stir in cheese until melted. Add
sauce to macaroni and mix well. Microwave at Medium
High 6 to 8 minutes or until hot. Stir twice during
cooking. Sprinkle with paprika, if desired.

QUICK BACON AND CHEESE QUICHE

POWER LEVEL: HIGH   SERVES: 6
TOTAL COOKING TIME: 14 to 17 minutes

1 baked 9-inch pie shell
6 slices bacon, cooked and crumbled
1 cup shredded Cheddar cheese
1 can (3 oz.) French fried onion rings, chopped
2 cups half and half
3 drops tabasco sauce
1/4 tsp. nutmeg
4 eggs, beaten
Paprika

Sprinkle half of bacon, half of onion rings and 1 cup
cheese over bottom of baked pie shell. Mix together
half and half, tabasco sauce and nutmeg in a 1-quart
measure. Microwave on High for 2 to 3 minutes until
warm. Stir a small amount of cream into eggs and then
stir egg mixture into remaining hot cream. Gently pour
into shell. Sprinkle with remaining bacon, onions and
paprika. Microwave on High 12 to 14 minutes until
almost set. Rotate dish 1/2 turn every 3 minutes. Let
stand 5 to 10 minutes until center is set.

* FRESH VEGETABLES *

° Garden fresh vegetables cook more quickly than those purchased at the store.

° Put a lid or plastic wrap over vegetables to keep in the moisture.

° Potatoes and squash can be cooked whole without a covering. Be sure to prick in several places.

° Most vegetables cook on High power.

° Brown freckles on the "Veggies"? You have salted them directly. Remember salt is a drying agent and should be added to the cooking water. Other seasonings may be added as desired.

° Add 2 Tbsp. water to vegetables, unless recipe states otherwise.

° <u>Vegetables keep cooking!</u> Most vegetables need 3 to 5 minutes standing time to finish cooking and develop flavor.

° "Why are my vegetables tough?" You are probably overcooking. Certain vegetables such a green beans, carrots and lima beans tend to become tough during microwave cooking. Best to start these particular vegetables in 1/2 to 3/4 cup water. Microwave on High until boiling, then reduce power to Medium for 5 to 8 minutes or until tender. Lima beans will never be very good and fresh green beans are marginal.

° Whole or big chunky vegetables should be turned over half-way through cooking.

° The best way to have tender, evenly cooked vegetables is to cut them in small, uniform pieces.

75

° Broccoli and asparagus cook evenly when thick stem pieces are placed to the outside of the dish. The flower ends, which cook quickly, are arranged toward the center.

° MOST PEOPLE AGREE! Corn on the cob and zucchini are the best microwaved vegetables.

° Easily remove cabbage leaves for stuffed cabbage. Place a whole, cored cabbage in a pie plate. Add 2 Tbsp. water, cover with plastic wrap and Microwave on High for 8 to 9 minutes. Leaves should pull off easily.

° Although removing cabbage leaves is easy in the microwave, cooked stuffed cabbage rolls are more successful when done conventionally.

° To peel tomatoes with ease, place in the microwave for 10 seconds per tomato. Let stand a minute before peeling. Watch the timing or you'll make stewed tomatoes for dinner!

FROZEN AND CANNED VEGETABLES

° Frozen vegetables may be cooked in the oven-proof plastic pouch, box or freezer container (no metal containers). Remove any colored paper from around frozen boxes as dye may stain the bottom of the microwave.

° Slit frozen vegetable pouches so steam may escape.

° Place frozen vegetables with the icy side up in the dish.

° Stir or rotate vegetables for even cooking.

° Use only half the canned vegetable liquid for heating.

° Wish to use a temperature probe to heat vegetables? Probe setting to heat canned vegetables is 140° to 150°.

76

○ Remember to cook frozen vegetables with frozen vegetables, canned with canned and fresh with fresh. They have different cooking times.

○ WHEN COOKING VEGETABLES MADE WITH EGGS, CREAM OR SOUR CREAM; PREVENT CURDLING BY COOKING ON MEDIUM POWER.

○ Dry beans and peas should be pre-soaked. Fast cooking won't allow softening and rehydration time.

○ Pick small quantities of garden vegetables to microwave blanch and freeze.

* RICE *

○ Get your rice on the right wave-length! Rice takes almost the same cooking time as the top of the stove but it's terrific.

○ Rice is nice when cooked and served in the same casserole.

○ For white, fluffy rice add 1/2 tsp. lemon juice to 2 cups of water.

○ WHEN COOKING LONG-GRAIN RICE, USE 2 CUPS WATER TO 1 CUP RICE. LESS WATER IS NEEDED IN A MICROWAVE.

○ Rice needs to stand 5 to 10 minutes until water is completely absorbed. Don't be tempted to put the rice back in the oven for longer cooking.

○ Toss cooked rice lightly to prevent mush.

* PASTA *

° Some pasta is very good cooked in the microwave. Other pasta resembles a recipe for wallpaper paste.

° The best pasta is spaghetti or linquine and lasagna noodles. <u>Thin</u> egg noodles and macaroni work well. <u>Skip</u> medium and large egg noodles and manicotti shells.

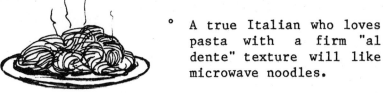

° A true Italian who loves pasta with a firm "al dente" texture will like microwave noodles.

° Place 1/2 pound spaghetti or lasagna noodles (no more than 7 noodles) in 6 cups of hot water in a 12 x 8 inch dish. Add 1 Tbsp. oil and 1/2 tsp. salt. Cover with plastic wrap and Microwave on High 11 to 14 minutes. Rearrange after 6 minutes.

THREE "SUPER SAVER" IDEAS

A. Dry herbs and spices in a microwave

Select parsley, thyme, celery leaves, chives or a variety of herbs. Wash and pat them dry and remove leaves from stems. Spread 1-1/2 to 2 cups of leaves on a double thickness of paper towels. Microwave 3 to 6 minutes on High, stirring frequently. Timing differs with selected herb. Do not overcook as the dried leaves can burn. Herbs will be dry as paper and crispy. Store in a cool dry place.

B. Dry vegetables and fruit in a microwave

Foods dry best in a food dryer or convection oven but they can be done in small amounts in a microwave. The food is dried and then rehydrated with liquid later.

MUSHROOMS - clean, slice and arrange on double thickness of paper towels. Microwave on Medium for 7 to 11 minutes, rearranging mushrooms once. Time varies according to the amount and size of mushrooms. Dry thoroughly and store in an air-tight container.

LEMON or ORANGE RIND - Place grated rind (not white membrane) of lemon or orange on a double layer of paper towels. Spread evenly. Microwave on Defrost (30%) for 30 minutes, rearranging frequently. Rind should be hard after cooling. Store in air-tight container.

OTHER FOODS that can be dried in a microwave are: apples, peaches, carrots, peas and onions.

C. Blanch Vegetables for the freezer in a microwave

Blanching is an easy way to freeze fresh vegetables in a large quantity or a few servings. Wash, peel and slice vegetables. Place a quart or a pound of vegetables in a casserole. Add 1/2 cup water and do not salt. Cover dish tightly. Microwave on High for 3 to 6 minutes, until vegetables are bright in color. Drain and plunge into ice water immediately to stop cooking. Blot with towels to remove excess moisture. Package in boil-bags or freezing containers.

79

ACORN SQUASH WITH APPLE FILLING

POWER LEVEL: HIGH   SERVES: 4
TOTAL COOKING TIME: 16 to 19 minutes

2 medium acorn squash
2 medium apples, sliced
1/2 cup packed brown sugar
1/4 cup butter
Cinnamon
Chopped walnuts or pecans (optional)

Pierce skin of squash to allow steam to escape. Microwave on High 11 to 13 minutes or until almost tender.
Turn squash over halfway through cooking. Cut squash
in half and remove seeds. Place open side up on a 2-
quart utility dish or a platter. Fill centers of
squash with apples. Top each with 2 Tbsp. brown sugar,
1 Tbsp. butter and sprinkle with cinnamon. Microwave
on High 5 to 6 minutes until apples are tender. Top
with nuts.

VARIATIONS: Delicious acorn squash fillings are
             orange marmelade, cranberry sauce or
             drained canned fruit with brown sugar.

SCALLOPED CORN PUDDING

POWER LEVEL: MEDIUM HIGH   SERVES: 4
TOTAL COOKING TIME: 16 to 20 minutes

1 can (16 oz.) cream style corn
2 eggs, slightly beaten
1/2 cup milk
1 Tbsp. onion, chopped
1 Tbsp. sugar
3/4 cup cracker crumbs
2 Tbsp. butter or margarine, cut in pieces
Paprika
80

Combine corn, eggs, milk, onion, sugar and cracker crumbs in a 1-1/2 quart casserole. Dot with butter and sprinkle with paprika. Microwave on Medium High 16 to 20 minutes or until knife inserted near edge comes out clean. Rotate dish halfway during cooking. Let stand 10 minutes.

ITALIAN STUFFED TOMATOES

POWER LEVEL: HIGH   SERVES: 4
TOTAL COOKING TIME: 7 to 8 minutes

4 medium tomatoes
2 cups chopped fresh mushrooms
1/4 cup onions, chopped
1/4 cup green peppers, chopped
2 Tbsp. butter or margarine
1/3 cup flavored bread crumbs, Italian style
1/4 tsp. salt
Dash of pepper
1 egg, beaten
1 cup mozzarella or Cheddar cheese

Remove stem ends of tomatoes and scoop out center pulp and seeds. Place tomatoes in pie plate or 8-inch dish. Place mushrooms, onions, green pepper and butter in a 1-quart casserole. Saute in Microwave on High 3 to 4 minutes. Stir in bread crumbs, salt, pepper, egg and 3/4 cup of cheese. Cover with plastic wrap. Microwave on High 4 minutes, rotating dish 1/2 turn halfway through cooking. Sprinkle remaining 1/4 cup cheese on top of tomatoes. Let stand, covered, 2 to 3 minutes.

NOTE: Overly ripe tomatoes will cook faster. Over-
      cooking will cause tomatoes to lose shape.

CREAMY SEASONED BRUSSEL SPROUTS

POWER LEVEL: HIGH   SERVES: 4
TOTAL COOKING TIME: 7-1/2 to 10-1/2 minutes

---

1 package (10 oz.) frozen Brussel sprouts
1/4 cup water
2 Tbsp. butter or margarine
1/2 tsp. lemon juice
1/4 tsp. celery salt
1/4 tsp. chopped chives
1 package (3 oz.) cream cheese, cut in 1/4 inch cubes

Place brussel sprouts and water in a 1-quart casserole. Cover tightly and Microwave on High for 6 to 8 minutes until tender. Drain. Add butter, lemon juice, salt and chives to hot sprouts. Mix well. Microwave on High, uncovered, for 1-1/2 to 2-1/2 minutes until bubbly. Spread cream cheese cubes over brussel sprouts. Cover and let stand 3 minutes. Toss gently before serving.

CABBAGE IN SOUR CREAM

POWER LEVEL: HIGH AND MEDIUM   SERVES: 4 to 6
TOTAL COOKING TIME: 11 to 14 minutes

---

1 small head of cabbage, finely shredded
1/4 cup onion, chopped
1/4 cup water
1 tsp. salt
1/8 tsp. pepper
1/4 cup butter, melted
1 cup sour cream
1 Tbsp. dill weed

Combine cabbage, onion, water and salt in a 2-quart casserole. Cover tightly and Microwave on High 9 to 11 minutes. Stir cabbage after 5 minutes cooking time. Drain off liquid. Stir in pepper, butter, sour cream and dill weed. Microwave on Medium 2 to 3 minutes until warm.
82

GLAZED CARROTS AND ORANGES

POWER SETTING: HIGH   SERVES: 4
TOTAL COOKING TIME: 8 to 10 minutes

1 can (11 oz.) drained mandarin oranges (save 1/4 cup
    juice)
1/4 cup mandarin orange juice
1/4 tsp. salt
3 or 4 carrots, sliced in thin rounds
1-1/2 Tbsp. butter or margarine
1/3 cup brown sugar
1 Tbsp. grated orange rind

Combine orange juice, salt and carrots in a 1-1/2 quart
casserole. Cover tightly and Microwave on High 4 to 5
minutes. Stir in butter, sugar and orange rind. Cover
tightly and Microwave on High 3 to 4 minutes until carrots are glazed. Gently stir in oranges and Microwave
1 minute on High to warm.

ZUCCHINI SUPREME

POWER LEVEL: MEDIUM HIGH   SERVES: 4 to 6
TOTAL COOKING TIME: 12 to 16 mintues

4 cups zucchini (2 medium), cut in chunks
1/2 cup onions, chopped
1-1/2 cups grated Cheddar cheese
1 jar (2 oz.) chopped pimiento, drained
1/4 tsp. salt
Dash of pepper
4 eggs, well beaten

Combine zucchini and onions in a 10 x 6 x 2 inch dish.
Cover tightly and Microwave on High for 4 to 6 minutes.
Drain. Add cheese, pimiento, salt and pepper. Stir
mixture well. Pour eggs over ingredients. Microwave on
Medium, covered with waxed paper, for 8 to 10 minutes
until center is set. Stir gently after 4 minutes cooking time. Let stand 2 to 3 minutes.

83

GREEN BEANS IN PARMESAN SAUCE

POWER LEVEL: HIGH and MEDIUM   SERVES: 4
TOTAL COOKING TIME: 15 to 17 minutes

1 package (9 or 10 oz.) frozen green beans
1/4 cup water
1/4 cup mayonnaise
1 egg, beaten
1/3 cup grated Parmesan cheese
2 Tbsp. butter, melted
1/2 tsp. minced onion
1/4 tsp. mustard (optional)
1/4 cup toasted slivered almonds

Place green beans and water in a 1-quart casserole. Microwave, covered, on High for 10 to 12 minutes. Break apart halfway through cooking. Drain. Mix together mayonnaise, egg, cheese, butter, minced onion and mustard. Pour over beans and mix well. Microwave on Medium for 4 minutes. Stir and sprinkle with almonds. Microwave on Medium 1 minute more.

CRUNCHY PARMESAN POTATOES

POWER LEVEL: HIGH   SERVES: 4
TOTAL COOKING TIME: 8 to 11 minutes

3 Tbsp. butter or margarine
1/2 cup cornflake crumbs or seasoned dry bread crumbs
1/4 cup Parmesan cheese
1 tsp. minced onion
1/4 tsp. salt
1/4 tsp. paprika
4 medium sized potatoes, cut into 4 lengthwise sections (peeling is optional)

Place butter in a 12 x 8 inch baking dish. Microwave on High for 1 minute until butter is melted. Combine crumbs, Parmesan cheese, minced onion, salt and paprika in a small bowl. Coat potatoes with butter and roll in crumb mixture. Place single layer in baking dish. Cover with paper towel and Microwave on High 8 to 11 minutes. Halfway through cooking, remove paper towel and rearrange potatoes. Let stand, uncovered, 10 minutes before serving.

PIZZA POTATOES

POWER LEVEL: HIGH   SERVES: 6
TOTAL COOKING TIME: 21 to 26 minutes

---

4 to 5 medium potatoes, peeled and sliced
1/4 cup water
1 pound ground beef
2 cans (8 oz. each) tomato sauce
1/4 tsp. Italian seasonings
3 to 4 oz. sliced pepperoni
1 cup (4 oz.) shredded mozzarella cheese

Combine potato slices and water in a 12 x 8 inch baking dish. Cover tightly. Microwave on High for 10 to 12 minutes, or until tender. Drain potatoes and let stand. Crumble ground beef in 1-quart casserole and Microwave on High 5 to 6 minutes or until meat is no longer pink. Drain and break up meat. Stir in tomato sauce and seasoning. Pour meat sauce over potatoes. Arrange pepperoni evenly on top and sprinkle with cheese. Microwave, uncovered, 6 to 8 minutes until heated through. Rotate dish once during cooking.

CURRIED CAULIFLOWER

POWER LEVEL: HIGH   SERVES: 4 to 6
TOTAL COOKING TIME: 10-1/2 to 14-1/2 minutes

1 medium head cauliflower
1/4 cup water
1 cup medium white sauce (page 116)
1/4 cup sweet pickles, chopped or relish
1/4 cup butter or margarine, melted
1 cup dry bread crumbs
1/2 tsp. sweet basil, dried parsley or desired herb

Wash cauliflower and section into flowerettes. Place cauliflower and water in a 2-quart casserole. Cover tightly and Microwave on High 6 to 8 minutes until tender. Drain. To 1 cup of medium white sauce add pickles or relish. Pour over cauliflower and stir. Combine melted butter, crumbs and desired herb. Sprinle over cauliflower and Microwave 1 to 2 minutes on High.

VARIATION:

DEVILED CAULIFLOWER - Add 1 can (4-1/2 oz.) deviled ham to cooked white sauce along with pickles or relish.

QUICK CUISINE RICE

Combine 1 cup instant rice, 1 package (10 oz.) frozen Japanese, Chinese or Hawaiian vegetables, thawed, 1 cup chicken bouillon and 1 can (4 oz.) tiny shrimp. Cover and Microwave 5 to 7 minutes on High. Stir twice during cooking. Add soy sauce for flavor, if desired.

RICE PILAFF

POWER LEVEL: HIGH and MEDIUM   SERVES: 4 to 6
TOTAL COOKING TIME: 22 to 25 minutes

1/2 cup celery, diced   1/2 tsp. salt
1 cup long grain rice   1/4 tsp. tarragon
2 Tbsp. butter or margarine   1/4 cup water
1/2 cup onions, finely chopped
1/2 cup fresh parsley, chopped
1 can (14 oz.) chicken broth or bouillon

Combine all ingredients in a 2-quart casserole. Cover tightly and Microwave 7 minutes on High or until boiling. Stir. Cover and Microwave on Medium 15 to 18 minutes. Let stand 10 minutes, covered, until liquid is absorbed.

SPANISH RICE

POWER LEVEL: HIGH and MEDIUM   SERVES: 4 to 5
TOTAL COOKING TIME: 22 to 25 minutes

---

6 strips of bacon, cooked and crumbled
1 cup long grain rice
1/2 cup onions, chopped
1/4 cup green pepper, chopped
1 can (16 oz.) tomatoes, undrained
1 cup tomato juice
1/4 cup parsley, chopped
1 tsp. salt
Dash of pepper
1/2 tsp. Worcestershire sauce

Combine all ingredients in a 2-quart casserole. Mix well and cover tightly. Microwave on High for 7 minutes or until boiling. Stir. Cover and Microwave on Medium 15 to 18 minutes. Let stand, covered, until liquid is absorbed.

NOODLES ROMANOFF

POWER LEVEL: HIGH AND MEDIUM   SERVES: 6
TOTAL COOKING TIME: 19 to 21 minutes

---

1 package (7 to 8 oz) narrow noodles
4 cups very hot water
1 Tbsp oil
1 tsp. salt
1 cup cottage cheese
1 cup sour cream
1/4 cup finely chopped green onions
1 glove garlic, minced
2 Tbsp. butter or margarine
1 tsp. Worcestershire sauce
Parmesan cheese
Paprika

Place noodles, hot water, oil and salt in a 3-quart casserole. Cover tightly. Microwave on High for 10 minutes, stirring twice. Noodles will be softened but not
completely cooked. Drain and rinse with hot water, if
desired. Add cheese, sour cream, onions, garlic, butter and Worcestershire sauce. Mix well. Cover and
Microwave on Medium for 9 to 11 minutes, until hot and
bubbly. Stir once after 4 minutes. Sprinkle with Parmesan cheese and paprika.

NOTE: Use spinach noodles instead of regular noodles
        for a delicious change.

* QUICK BREADS *

° LET'S FACE IT, yeast bread bakes best in a conventional oven.

° WHEN CHOOSING TO MICROWAVE YEAST DOUGH - use yeast dough recipes especially designed for microwaving.

° Microwave yeast bread recipes are good for soft sandwich bread and for toasting.

° Breads do not brown and need cosmetic aid.

° Bake all microwave bread products uncovered.

° A microwave can aid you in slightly thawing frozen yeast bread dough. Place dough in a loaf pan, covered with a damp cloth and then a dry cloth. Microwave on Low for 2 minutes. Let bread rest 2 minutes and then Microwave another 2 minutes. Be careful that bread doesn't start to cook.

° Microwave books will tell you how to proof dough in the microwave. Apparently, it works for many people. My attempts have not been successful as the dough starts to cook.

° Quick breads are fast and tasty but will not be brown or crusty. Add brown sugar, cinnamon, nuts or toasted coconut as topping.

° Loaves of quick bread such as dark zucchini or nut bread are attractive and can be sliced for sandwiches.

° Microwave breads, like cakes, dry out quickly and keep only a few days. Store in air-tight plastic wrap or foil in refrigerator. Breads freeze well.

° Big pizza eaters should invest in a pizza wheel or pizza dish designed especially for pizza in the microwave. They do a good job.

° When reheating pizza - remember to remove the cardboard bottom. Pizza can sometimes be soggy enough without eating cardboard.

CORN BREAD

POWER LEVEL: MEDIUM HIGH   SERVES: 1 (9-inch ring)
TOTAL COOKING TIME: 8 to 10 minutes

1 cup yellow corn meal
1 cup all-purpose flour
2 Tbsp. sugar
4 tsp. baking powder
1/2 tsp. salt
1 egg
1 cup milk
1/2 cup cooking oil

Sift together corn meal, flour, sugar, baking powder and salt. Add eggs, milk and cooking oil. Beat with rotary beater 1 minute until smooth. Pour batter into a 9-inch round or ring mold pan. Microwave on Medium High for 8 to 10 minutes, rotating dish 1/4 turn every 3 minutes. A toothpick inserted in the center should come out clean. Let stand on cooling rack 5 minutes before serving.

Makes 1 (9-inch) ring

VARIATIONS:

MEXICAN CORN BREAD - Add 1 (12 oz.) can drained Mexicorn niblets and 1/4 tsp. chili powder to batter before baking.

COUNTRY CHEESE CORN BREAD - Add 1 cup shredded Cheddar cheese and 1/2 tsp. chili powder to batter before baking.

HEARTY SAUSAGE CORN BREAD - Add 1/2 pound cooked, crumbled bulk sausage to batter before baking.

EASY APPLESAUCE MUFFINS

POWER LEVEL: HIGH   SERVES: 12 to 16 Muffins
TOTAL COOKING TIME: FOLLOW CHART

---

1 box (13-14 oz.) applesauce-raisin snack cake mix
1 cup water
2 Tbsp. butter or margarine, melted
1/3 cup sugar

In mixing bowl, combine cake mix and water. Spoon 2 to 3 Tbsp. batter into microwave proof muffin trays lined with 2 paper liners. Arrange 6 muffins in a circle (if using lined custard cups). Microwave on High following the muffin timing chart. Rearrange and rotate muffins after half the cooking time. Place on cooling rack. Repeat directions for remaining muffin mix. When cooled, brush top of muffins with melted butter and sprinkle with sugar.

MUFFIN TIMING CHART ON HIGH POWER

1 muffin - 20 to 40 seconds
2 muffins - 1/2 to 1-1/2 minutes
4 muffins - 2 to 2-1/2 minutes
6 muffins - 3 to 4 minutes

YOGURT COFFEE CAKE

POWER LEVEL: HIGH   SERVES: 1 (9-inch) Cake
TOTAL COOKING TIME: 6 to 8 minutes

1 carton (8 oz.) plain or flavored yogurt
3/4 cup sugar
1/4 cup butter or margarine, melted
2 eggs
1 Tbsp. grated lemon peel
1-1/2 cups flour
3/4 tsp. soda
1/4 cup finely chopped nuts
1/4 cup sugar
1 tsp. cinnamon
2 Tbsp. butter or margarine, melted

Stir together yogurt, 3/4 cup sugar and butter until
well blended. With a wooden spoon, beat in eggs and
lemon peel until smooth. Stir in flour and soda. Blend
until just smooth, do not overbeat. Pour batter into
a 9-inch round cake pan. Mix the nuts, 1/4 cup sugar
and cinnamon together. Sprinkle over the batter
evenly. Drizzle melted butter over batter. Microwave
on High 6 to 8 minutes, turning twice during cooking.
Cake is done when it pulls away from the edge of the
pan. It may be slightly wet on the top. Let stand 20
minutes before serving.

NOTE: All flavors or plain yogurt can be used. Lemon,
        orange or coffee flavored yogurt are delicious.

* CAKES AND COOKIES *

° FORGET ABOUT MICROWAVING angelfood and chiffon cakes. They need hot air for crisping.

° Cakes bake best in round dishes.

° Make your own ringmold. Place a 4 or 5 inch drinking glass open side up in the center of the dish. Use a glass in the center of a 3-quart mixing bowl or casserole to make a bundt pan.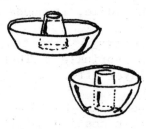

° Shield corners with small pieces of foil when using a square or oblong cake dish.

° Setting a cake on an inverted saucer during cooking helps to evenly microwave the cake bottom.

° Microwave cakes are funny looking when compared to conventional cakes - but they are delicious. The cakes do not brown and appear undercooked.

° "My cake grew and grew. In fact, it grew out of the pan and all over the oven." Next time use a larger pan and fill no more than 1/2 full. Microwave cakes have more volume because there is no hot air to form a crust.

° Plain box cakes rise higher and are lighter in texture than cakes containing pudding.

° Chocolate cakes cook a bit faster than yellow or white ones.

° Does the cake have a puddle in the middle? Microwave cakes often have moist, doughy areas on the top. Touch the area lightly for doneness. If the cake beneath is firm, it's done. If the batter is a puddle, it needs a little more time.

° To dry a cake top, either blot with a paper towel or sprinkle 1 Tbsp. graham cracker crumbs on each layer after cooking.

° Best not to flour or grease the baking dish as a thin coating will remain on the cake. Line the bottom of layer cake pans with waxed paper for easy removal.

° Cake too moist? For cakes with a large amount of moisture, reduce liquid by 1/4 next time.

° "In 2 days, my cake was all dried out!" Microwave cakes do become stale faster than conventional cakes. Adding 2 Tbsp. oil to 1 layer cake batter and 3 Tbsp. oil to large cake batter helps retain moisture. Store covered. (to keep cakes fresh, put an apple cut in half in the storage container)

° "I want to rotate the cake, will it fall?" No, open the door, and even talk to the cake for a few minutes and it won't fall.

° Defrosting tip. A frozen cake can be defrosted at Medium for 3 to 4 minutes. It will be cool and should cut easily.

° THE CAKE IS SUPPOSED TO LOOK LIKE A CAR CLEANING SPONGE. DON'T PUT IT BACK IN THE OVEN!

** EASY CAKE TOPPING: Combine 3 Tbsp. butter or margarine, 1/2 cup brown sugar and 1 Tbsp. milk in a glass mixing bowl. Microwave on High 1 to 2 minutes until bubbly. Stir in 1/2 cup coconut and 1/4 cup chopped nuts. Spread onto cake using a fork. Makes topping for 1 layer.

° A basic cake or pudding bundt cake can be changed
with the addition of a cup of chocolate chips,
chopped fruit and nuts or 1/2 inch squares of plain
cranberry sauce. Substitute wine, coffee, or juice
instead of water. Glaze by sprinkling dried fruit
drink mix or colored jello over warm cake.

CUP CAKES ARE FAST AND EASY

° Make cupcake holders from styrofoam or paper cups.
Place 2 cupcake liners inside the cups for more
support and to absorb moisture. Fill 1/3 full,
cupcakes rise high.

° Expect cupcake tops to be moist. Immediately after
cooking, remove cupcakes from holders and let cool
on a wire rack.

° Arrange cupcakes in a ring on a paper towel or
round dish. Turn the paper or dish to rotate the
cakes.

° <u>Children's fun.</u> Use flat-bottom ice cream cones
when microwaving cup cakes. Fill cones 1/3 full
with batter. Follow muffin timing chart. (page 91).

COOKIES

° Bar-type cookies are better in a microwave than
drop cookies. Drop cookies cook too quickly. They
tend to crumble.

° Place most cookie batters in a 12 x 8 dish and bake
on High 5 to 7 minutes. Cut into squares when cool.

° Do not cover baked goods when microwaving.

° Use foil strips to cover the corners of baking
dishes to prevent overcooking the edges.

INDIVIDUAL BAKED CUSTARDS

POWER LEVEL: HIGH and LOW   SERVES: 4
TOTAL COOKING TIME: 16 to 22 minutes

1-3/4 cups milk   1/4 tsp. salt
3 eggs   1 tsp. vanilla
1/4 cup sugar   Dash cinnamon or nutmeg

In a 2 cup glass measure, Microwave milk on High for 3
to 4 minutes until scalded. Beat together eggs, sugar,
salt and vanilla in a bowl. Gradually pour hot milk
into egg mixture, stirring continuously. Pour into 4
(6 oz. size) custard cups. Cover with plastic wrap or
tight lids. Microwave on Low for 13 to 18 minutes,
rearranging cups halfway through cooking. If some custards are done before others, remove as they finish
cooking. Sprinkle with cinnamon or nutmeg and chill,
uncovered, for 1 hour.

BREAD PUDDING

POWER LEVEL: HIGH and MEDIUM   SERVES: 6
TOTAL COOKING TIME: 14 to 18 minutes

2 cups dry bread cubes (3-4 slices)   2-1/4 cups milk
1/2 cup brown sugar   1/4 cup butter
1/2 cup raisins   3 eggs, beaten
1 tsp. cinnamon   1 tsp. vanilla
1/4 tsp. salt
1/2 tsp nutmeg

In a 2-quart casserole, toss bread, sugar, raisins, cinnamon and salt. Set aside. Add milk and butter to a 1-
quart measure. Microwave on High 4 minutes until milk
is warm but not boiling. Stir in eggs and vanilla. Pour
over bread and raisin mixture and let stand 3 minutes to
absorb moisture. Microwave on Medium for 10 to 14 minutes, rotating dish 1/2 turn after 6 minutes. Let stand
10 to 15 minutes until center is firm. Sprinkle with
cinnamon, if desired. Serve warm or cool.

96

CHOCOLATE CHIP COOKIES

POWER LEVEL: MEDIUM   SERVES: 2-1/2 dozen
TOTAL COOKING TIME: 2 to 4 minutes

1/2 cup butter or margarine
2/3 cup brown sugar
1 egg
1 tsp. vanilla
1 tsp. soda
1/2 tsp. salt
1-1/2 cups all-purpose flour
1/2 to 1 cup chocolate chips
1/2 cup nuts, chopped (optional)

Cream together butter and sugar until fluffy. Add egg
and vanilla. Mix well. Gradually add soda, salt and
flour, blending thoroughly. Mix in chocolate chips
and nuts. Drop 6 to 8 rounded teaspoons of dough in
a wide circle on waxed or parchment paper. Place paper on a dinner or paper plate for stability. Microwave on Medium 2 to 4 minutes until dry on top. Rotate dish 1/2 turn every 30 seconds. Microwave cookies
will not have a browned top. After cooling, frost or
add powdered sugar, if desired.

NOTE: Place above recipe in a 8-inch round or square
       dish for bar-type cookies. Microwave at Med-
       ium High for 6 to 8 minutes, rotating dish 1/4
       turn every 2 minutes.

CHOCOLATE BROWNIES – ONE DISH

POWER LEVEL: HIGH   SERVES: 1 dozen
TOTAL COOKING TIME: 6 to 7 minutes

1/2 cup butter or margarine
1 cup sugar
2 eggs
1 tsp. vanilla
1/2 tsp. salt
1/2 tsp. baking powder
3/4 cup all purpose flour
1/2 cup cocoa
1/2 cup chopped nuts (optional)

Place butter in 8-inch round baking dish. Microwave on
High 1 minute or until melted. Add sugar, eggs, and
vanilla. Mix thoroughly. Blend in remaining dry ingredients and mix well. Sprinkle nuts over batter. Microwave on High for 6 to 7 minutes or until top appears dry
and springs back when lightly touched. Rotate dish 1/2
turn twice during cooking. Let stand until cool.

VARIATION:

BUTTERSCOTCH BROWNIES – substitute 3/4 cup brown sugar
for 1 cup granulated sugar and eliminate cocoa.

CHEERY BARS

POWER LEVEL: HIGH and MEDIUM   SERVES: 12 to 16 bars
TOTAL COOKING TIME: 5 to 9 minutes

1 bag (14 oz.) caramel candies
1/4 cup water
1/2 cup peanut butter
4 cups Cherrios cereal
1 cup salted peanuts

Topping: 1 cup chocolate chips
             3 Tbsp. peanut butter
             2 Tbsp. butter or margarine

Combine caramels, water and peanut butter in large mixing bowl. Microwave on High 3 to 5 minutes or until
melted, stirring after 2 minutes cooking time. Stir
in Cheerios and peanuts. Press into 13 x 9 or 12 x 8
baking dish. Place topping ingredients in small bowl.
Microwave on Medium 2 to 4 minutes until chips are
soft. Stir well and spread evenly over bars. Cool
and cut.

DREAM BARS

POWER LEVEL: MEDIUM   SERVES: 9 to 12 bars
TOTAL COOKING TIME: 11 to 15 minutes

6 Tbsp. butter or margarine   1 cup nuts, chopped
1/4 cup brown sugar   1 tsp. vanilla
1 cup all-purpose flour   1/2 tsp. baking powder
2 eggs   1/2 cup flaked coconut
1 cup brown sugar

Cream together butter and 1/4 sugar in a small mixing
bowl. Blend in flour until crumbly. Press into 8 or 9
inch baking dish. Microwave on Medium 4 to 5 minutes,
rotating dish 1/4 turn every 2 minutes. Combine eggs,
1 cup brown sugar, nuts, vanilla and baking powder.
Beat gently until well blended. Spread over crust.
Microwave on Medium 6 to 8 minutes or until center is
set. Rotate dish 1/4 turn every 2 minutes. Sprinkle
with coconut and Microwave on Medium for 1 to 2 minutes until set. Cool before cutting.

PINEAPPLE UPSIDE-DOWN CAKE

POWER LEVEL: HIGH   SERVES: 6
TOTAL COOKING TIME: 7 to 9 minutes

1/4 cup butter or margarine
1/2 cup brown sugar
1 can (8 oz.) sliced pineapple, reserve liquid
1/2 cup pineapple juice
4 maraschino cherries
4 nuts (optional)
1 package (9 oz.) yellow, spice or lemon cake mix

Place butter in an 8 or 9-inch cake dish. Microwave 1
minute on High until melted. Sprinkle sugar over butter
and stir until well mixed. Arrange pineapple slices,
cherries and nuts over syrup. Prepare cake mix according to package directions substituting fruit juice for
water. (add water to drained pineapple juice to make
1/2 cup, if necessary). Gently pour batter over fruit.
Microwave on High 6 to 8 minutes. Turn dish 1/2 turn
after 3 minutes cooking time. Let stand 5 minutes before inverting onto serving dish

NUT TORTE

POWER LEVEL: HIGH   SERVES: 1 (8-inch) cake
TOTAL COOKING TIME: 5 to 7 minutes

4 eggs
1/4 cup sugar
1/8 tsp. salt
1/3 cup sugar
1 tsp. vanilla
1 cup chopped nuts
1 cup vanilla wafer crumbs
1-1/4 tsp. baking powder
1/2 tsp. cinnamon

Separate eggs. In large bowl beat egg whites until foamy. Gradually beat in 1/4 cup sugar and salt until mixture is fluffy and holds soft peaks. In another bowl, beat egg yolks, 1/3 cup sugar and vanilla until pale yellow and thick. Fold yolk mixture into egg whites. Alternately fold in nuts, crumbs, baking powder and cinnamon. Spread batter into a greased 8-inch round dish. Microwave on High for 5 to 7 minutes, rotating dish 1/2 turn after 2 minutes. Glaze with Orange Liqueur Sauce or Orange Butter Sauce (page 120).

ORANGE LIQUEUR SAUCE: Add 4 Tbsp. Triple Sec, Cointreau or any other orange liqueur to cooked Orange Butter Sauce.

PETITE CHEESECAKES

POWER LEVEL: HIGH   SERVES: 18 to 24 Cheesecakes
TOTAL COOKING TIME: 4 to 5 minutes

---

18 to 24 vanilla wafers
2 packages (8 oz.) cream cheese, softened
3/4 cup sugar
2 eggs
1 Tbsp. lemon juice
1 tsp. vanilla
1 can (21 oz.) prepared cherry or blueberry
  pie filling

Place a vanilla wafer in the bottom of small custard cups or paper-lined muffin cups. In a microwave-proof bowl, beat cheese until smooth. Gradually blend in sugar and eggs. Stir in lemon juice and vanilla. Microwave on High 4 to 5 minutes until thickened, stirring twice during cooking. Spoon a rounded tablespoonful of cream cheese mixture onto each wafer and spread evenly. Top each with a spoonful of pie filling. Refrigerate until set, about 2-1/2 to 3 hours. (To easily remove the paper liners, partially freeze the cups until edges are firm). Remove papers and serve. Excellent for freezing.

CARROT CAKE

POWER LEVEL: HIGH   SERVES: 1 Layer Cake
TOTAL COOKING TIME: 6 to 7 minutes

3/4 cup sugar
1/2 cup cooking oil
1/2 tsp. vanilla
2 eggs
3/4 cup flour
1/2 tsp. salt
1 tsp. baking soda
1 tsp. cinnamon
1 cup grated raw carrots
1/4 cup chopped walnuts or raisins

Combine sugar, oil, vanilla and eggs in a large mixing bowl. Blend well. Add remaining ingredients and mix thoroughly. Pour into a 9-inch round or 8-inch square, greased baking dish. Microwave on High 6 to 7 minutes, rotating dish 1/2 turn after 3 minutes cooking time. Let stand on solid surface until cool. Frost with Cream Cheese Frosting, if desired.

* CREAM CHEESE FROSTING

Place 1 package (3 oz.) cream cheese, and 1/4 cup butter in a mixing bowl. Microwave on Medium 30 seconds to 1 minute until softened. Blend in 2 cups powdered sugar and 1 tsp. vanilla until light and fluffy. Makes 1-1/2 cups.

* PIES *

° Microwaved pie crust is tasty but does not brown. Add color and variety to crusts.

- Use whole wheat flour
- Chocolate crust is made by adding 1 Tbsp. sugar and 2 Tbsp. cocoa to dough
- Spice crust is made by adding 1 Tbsp. cinnamon and 1/4 tsp. ginger or nutmeg to dough
- Cheese crust is made by substituting 1/2 cup Cheddar cheese in place of butter or shortening
- Coconut-Nut is made by adding 1/2 cup toasted coconut and 1/4 cup chopped nuts to pastry

° Bake all microwave pie shells before filling.

° When making pie crust, handle the dough as little as possible.

° Add 3 to 4 drops of yellow food coloring to pastry for color.

° Sprinkle cinnamon and sugar combination on the top of pies.

° The best microwaved crust is struesel, cookie or cracker crumbs or crumble-type pastry.

° To prevent microwave crust from sticking to the pan after cooking, lightly grease the pie plate with salad dressing before adding pastry.

° Pinch a crimped rim around the unbaked pie shell and hook each pinched section under the rim to avoid a shrinking crust.

° Prevent a shrinking pie crust by chilling the pie crust after mixing. Makes it easier to handle.

° Double crust pies are not too successful in a microwave. For top crust, try using pastry cutouts or lattice work.

Combine microwave and conventional oven for great pie making

° Make pies in a dish for both uses.

UNFROZEN PIES - Microwave on High 10 to 12 minutes. Place in preheated conventional oven at 425° for an additional 15 to 18 minutes until juices bubble.

FROZEN PIES - Microwave on High 15 to 17 minutes. Place in preheated conventional oven at 425° for 18 to 20 minutes.

° Pie's all done but the center is soup? Place small strips of foil over the cooked sections and continue microwaving for a few minutes until center is completed. This hint works for all foods like cakes, casseroles and puddings that suffer from "soupy centers".

PUMPKIN PIE

POWER LEVEL: MEDIUM   SERVES: 1 (9 or 10-
TOTAL COOKING TIME: 26 to 32 minutes   inch) pie

---

1 (9 or 10-inch) baked pie shell	1 Tbsp. flour
2 eggs	1 tsp. cinnamon
1 cup packed brown sugar	1/2 tsp. salt
1 can (15 oz.) cooked pumpkin	1/2 tsp. nutmeg
1 can (13 oz.) evaporated milk	1/4 tsp. ginger

Combine all filling ingredients in a 2-quart casserole. Mix until smooth. Microwave mixture in casserole at Medium for 13 to 15 minutes, stirring frequently. Pour into pie shell. Microwave at Medium for 13 to 15 minutes for a 9-inch pie; 15 to 17 minutes for a 10-inch pie. Rotate pie 1/4 turn every 4 minutes. The center will be slightly soft. Let stand 15 minutes.

CRACKER CRUMB CRUST

POWER LEVEL: HIGH   SERVES: 1 (9-inch) pie shell
TOTAL COOKING TIME: 2-1/2 to 3 minutes

1/3 cup butter or margarine
1-1/4 cups fine cookie or graham cracker crumbs
2 Tbsp. granulated or brown sugar

Melt butter in a 9-inch pie pan on High 1 minute. Stir in crumbs and sugar. Save 2 Tbsp. crumb mixture for garnish. Press firmly and evenly into bottom and sides of dish. Microwave on High 1-1/2 to 2 minutes, rotating dish 1/2 turn after 1 minute.

VARIATIONS: Use chocolate wafers, gingersnaps, vanilla wafers, pecan sandy cookies or cereal crumbs.

CRUNCHY NUT PASTRY

POWER LEVEL: HIGH   SERVES: 1 (9-inch) pie
TOTAL COOKING TIME: 6 minutes   shell

---

1 cup flour
1/2 cup light brown sugar
1/2 cup butter or margarine
1 cup chopped pecans or walnuts

Cut butter into flour and brown sugar with pastry blender. When mixture is crumbly, mix in nuts. Place in 9-inch pie plate and Microwave on High for 4 minutes, stirring every 1 or 2 minutes. Press mixture evenly into bottom and sides of pie plate. Microwave on High 2 minutes, until set. Rotate dish 1/4 turn after 1 minute. Cool before filling.

SOUR CREAM APPLE PIE

POWER LEVEL: HIGH   SERVES: 1 (9-inch) pie
TOTAL COOKING TIME: 7 to 8-1/2 minutes

1 (9-inch) baked pastry shell
4 cups peeled, sliced cooking apples
2/3 cup sugar
1 Tbsp. flour
1/2 tsp. cinnamon
1/2 cup sour cream
1 cup Butter Streusel Topping* (below)

Prepare a 9-inch baked pastry shell. Combine apples,
sugar, flour, cinnamon and sour cream. Spoon mixture
into pastry shell. Top with crumb topping, covering
apples completely. Microwave on High 7 to 8-1/2 minutes or until apples are tender. For extra browning,
place pie under broiler for a few minutes, if desired.
Let stand 5 minutes.

* BUTTER STREUSEL TOPPING

1 cup all-purpose flour
1/4 cup plus 2 Tbsp. butter or margarine
2 Tbsp. brown or granulated sugar
1/2 tsp. salt
1/2 tsp. cinnamon

Cut butter into flour, sugar, salt and cinnamon until
fine particles form. Sprinkly on top of fruit pie or
dessert. Bake as directed in recipe.

PUDDING CREAM PIE

POWER LEVEL: HIGH   SERVES: 1 (9-inch) pie
TOTAL COOKING TIME: 6-1/2 to 9-1/2 minutes

---

1 (9-inch) baked pie shell
1/2 to 3/4 cup sugar
3 Tbsp. cornstarch
1/4 tsp. salt
2 cups milk
3 egg yolks, slightly beaten
2 Tbsp. butter or margarine
1 tsp. vanilla

In a 1-quart casserole, mix together sugar, cornstarch and salt. Stir in milk gradually until smooth. Microwave on High 5 to 7 minutes until mixture is thickened. Stir every 2 minutes during cooking so lumps do not form. Stir a small amount of hot mixture into beaten egg yolks. Then stir egg mixture into hot pudding, mixing well. Microwave on High 1-1/2 to 2-1/2 minutes until pudding starts to boil rapidly and is thick. Stir once. Blend in butter and vanilla. Pour into pie shell and refrigerate. Use within 2 days. Top with merinque if desired.

VARIATIONS:

CHOCOLATE CREAM PIE: Add 2 squares (1 oz. each) unsweetened chocolate along with milk. Increase sugar to 1 cup. If mixture is not smooth, beat before adding egg yolks.

FROTHY MALLOW PIE

POWER LEVEL: HIGH   SERVES: 1 (9-inch) pie
TOTAL COOKING TIME: 2 to 3 minutes

1 crumb (9-inch) pie shell
1 package (10 oz.) large marshmallows
1/2 cup milk
1 cup whipping cream, whipped
Flavoring and variation ingredients

Place marshmallows and milk in a 3-quart casserole. Cover tightly. Microwave on High 2 to 3 minutes until marshmallows melt and puff up.   Stir mixture until smooth and creamy.   Chill in refrigerator 30 to 40 minutes until thickened. Fold in whipped cream and ingredients for pie selection from below. Pour into crust and refrigerate several hours before serving.

VARIATIONS:

ORANGE PIE: Fold into pie, 1/2 cup orange juice and 1 Tbsp. grated orange peel. Add 2 to 3 drops orange food coloring for appearance, if desired.

CHOCOLATE-NUT PIE: Microwave 3 milk chocolate bars with almonds (1.15 oz. each) on High 1 to 2 minutes until melted. Fold into pie.

FRUIT PIE: Fold into pie, 1-1/2 cups peeled and sliced fruit.

GRASSHOPPER PIE: Fold into pie, 1/4 cup green creme de menthe and 2 Tbsp. white creme de cocoa. Garnish with whipped cream and slivered chocolate.

* CANDY *

° Save candy making for a "cool" day. In hot moist weather candy becomes sugary and sticky.

° Candy becomes so hot it can melt microwave-proof plastic dishes. Use sturdy glass or ceramic utensils that can withstand high temperatures.

° In fact, microwave candy stays hot three times long-er than regular candy. You can burn your mouth sneaking candy long after it is supposed to be cool.

° The best way to prevent candy from boiling over is to use a very large bowl and butter the inside edge to a depth of 2 inches.

° Luckily, microwave candy tends not to crystalize. If candy should "sugar", add a bit of water and bring to a boil again in the microwave.

° Chocolate burns easily! Use only pure chocolate for melting. Flavored bits contain parafin and will not melt correctly in a microwave.

° Chocolate squares can be melted until "just soft" in paper wrappers, seam side up. Melt chocolate bits until they are glossy but still hold shape. Stir until smooth.

° Add a little salt to recipes containing chocolate, it brings out the flavor.

PEANUT BRITTLE

POWER LEVEL: HIGH   SERVES: 1 pound
TOTAL COOKING TIME: 8 to 11 minutes

1 cup sugar   1 tsp. butter
1/2 cup white corn syrup   1 tsp. vanilla extract
1 cup roasted, salted peanuts 1 tsp. baking soda

Combine sugar and corn syrup in a 2-quart casserole.
Microwave 4 minutes on High. Stir in nuts. Microwave
3 to 5 minutes on High until light brown. Stir butter
and vanilla into syrup. Microwave on High 1 to 2
minutes more. Syrup will be very hot. Add soda and
stir until mixture is light and foamy. Pour onto
greased cookie sheet. Cool and break into pieces.

KIDS 2-MINUTE FUDGE

POWER LEVEL: HIGH   SERVES: 24 pieces
TOTAL COOKING TIME: 2 minutes

1 package (1 pound) confectioner's sugar
1/2 cup cocoa
1/4 tsp. salt
1/4 cup milk
1 tsp. vanilla
1/2 cup butter or margarine
1/2 cup chopped nuts or minature marshmallows
        (optional)

Mix sugar, cocoa, salt, milk and vanilla together. Dot
butter pieces onto sugar mixture. Microwave at High
for 2 minutes or until milk feels warm and most of butter is melted. Stir vigorously. Blend in nuts or
marshmallows. Spread evenly in waxed paper lined 8 x 8
inch dish. Refrigerate 1 hour. Cut into squares.

* FRUITS *

° Peachy idea. Heat one or more peaches on High for 20 seconds each. Let stand 3 minutes and peel easily.

° No need to peel apples. Microwaved apples keep their original bright color during cooking.

° Avacado not ripe? Microwave it for 2 minutes on Medium. Turn over once during heating.

° Fresh fruit desserts, like apples and pears, will hold shape when cooked on High power, uncovered.

° "Flaky" coconut lovers can toast coconut for pie shells or a garnish. Add 1 cup flaked coconut to 3 Tbsp. melted butter in a pie plate. Microwave on High 6 to 8 minutes, stirring twice, until brown.

° Quickly rehydrate dried fruits. Place raisins, prunes, or apricots in a bowl, barely covered with water or wine. Cover lightly with wax paper and Microwave on High for 5 minutes. Let stand 3 to 5 minutes to "plump".

° Chilly fruit juices can be warmed for 15 seconds on High. Frozen orange juice contains Vitamin C which is heat sensitive and should be only paritally thawed in the microwave 1 minute or less.

° Defrost a 10 to 16 oz. package or plastic pouch of frozen fruit on defrost power level for 5 to 8 minutes. Defrost fruit until cold, firm, and slightly icy. (Be sure to remove metal or foil from package)

BAKED APPLES

POWER LEVEL: HIGH

SERVES: 4

TOTAL COOKING TIME: 4 to 6 minutes

---

4 apples, cored
1/4 cup brown sugar
2 Tbsp. butter or margarine

Slice a thin circle of skin from the top of each apple.
Place apples in a 8 or 9-inch dish. Place a Tbsp. sugar
and 1/2 tsp. butter in each cavity. Sprinkle with cinnamon. Cover with waxed paper and Microwave 4 to 6 minutes on High or until tender. Let stand 3 to 5 minutes
before serving.

FRUIT COBBLER

POWER LEVEL: HIGH

SERVES: 6

TOTAL COOKING TIME: 10 to 11 minutes

---

1 can (20 to 22 oz.) prepared fruit pie filling
1 box (9 oz.) cake mix (yellow or spice)
1/4 cup butter or margarine, melted
2 Tbsp. brown sugar
1 tsp. cinnamon
1/4 cup chopped nuts

Spread pie filling evenly in a 8-inch round or square
dish. Sprinkle with dry cake mix. Drizzle butter over
top. Combine sugar, cinnamon and nuts. Sprinkle over
top of mixture. Microwave on High 10 to 11 minutes,
rotating dish 1/2 turn after 5 minutes. Let stand 10
minutes. Serve warm with ice cream or whipped cream.

APPLESAUCE

POWER LEVEL: HIGH   SERVES: 1 quart
TOTAL COOKING TIME: 8 to 10 minutes

8 cooking apples, peeled, cored and quartered
1/2 cup water
3/4 cup sugar
1/2 to 1 tsp. cinnamon
1/8 tsp. cloves or nutmeg (optional)

In a 2-quart casserole, place apples and water. Cover
tightly and Microwave on High 8 to 10 minutes or until
apples are tender. Add remaining ingredients and mash
or puree in blender. Store in freezer or refrigerator.

BANANA ROYALE

POWER LEVEL: HIGH   SERVES: 6 to 8
TOTAL COOKING TIME: 5 minutes

1/4 cup butter or margarine
1/3 cup brown sugar
1 tsp. grated orange peel
1/4 tsp. nutmeg
1/2 tsp. cinnamon
4 bananas, peeled and quartered
1/4 cup rum or orange liqueur
Vanilla ice cream

Melt butter 1 minute on High in a 1-1/2 quart casserole.
Stir in sugar, orange peel, nutmeg and cinnamon. Microwave 1 minute on High until sugar is dissolved. Add
bananas, stirring to coat. Microwave 3 minutes on high.
Stir once during cooking. Pour rum or liqueur into 1
cup measure. Heat on High 15 to 20 seconds. Pour 1 Tbsp.
liquid into a metal spoon. Pour remaining rum or liqueur over dessert. Ignite liquid in spoon and pour
over dessert. Serve over ice cream.

CHERRIES JUBILEE

POWER LEVEL: HIGH   SERVES: 4 to 6
TOTAL COOKING TIME: 5 minutes

1 can (1 lb.) pitted dark sweet cherries
2 tsp. cornstarch
1/4 cup sugar
1 tsp. lemon juice
1 tsp. grated lemon peel
Vanilla ice cream

Drain cherries, reserving liquid. In a 1-1/2 quart
casserole, combine cherry juice, cornstarch and sugar.
Microwave on High 3 minutes or until juice thickens,
stirring every minute. Stir in cherries, lemon juice
and lemon rind. Microwave on High 2 minutes until
mixture is hot. Serve over ice cream.

SPICY FRUIT COMPOTE

POWER LEVEL: HIGH   SERVES: 6 to 8
TOTAL COOKING TIME: 5 to 7 minutes

1/2 cup butter or margarine
3/4 cup brown sugar
1/2 tsp. cinnamon
1/4 tsp. ginger
1 Tbsp. grated orange peel
1 tsp. curry (optional)
1 can (13 oz.) pineapple chunks, drained
1 can (11 oz.) mandarin oranges, drained
1 can (16 oz.) sliced pineapple, drained
1 can (16 oz.) sliced pears, drained

In a 12 x 8 inch dish, melt butter on High for 1 minute.
Blend in sugar and spices. Add drained fruit and mix
well. Microwave on High, covered with wax paper, for
4 to 6 minutes. Stir once during cooking. Let stand
3 to 5 minutes. Serve hot or chilled.

* SAUCES *

- Advantages of microwave sauce — measure, mix and quickly cook in one container. No scorching, lumps or burned saucepans. Prepare in quantity and freeze.

- Prevent boil-overs! Use a sauce container twice the volume of required ingredients.

- "My sauce won't thicken." When adapting your own sauce recipe to the microwave, increase the amount of flour or cornstarch, maintaining the same liquid.

- Scald milk on LOW when preparing custards and delicate sauces.

- A glass measuring cup is a convenient sauce-maker.

- "But, I love my double-boiler." Throw the silly thing out! A microwave replaces double-boiler cooking.

- WOODEN SPOONS OR SCRAPERS MAY BE LEFT IN THE SAUCE (or in any casserole) DURING COOKING FOR EASY STIRRING. Beware of leaving plastic stirrers in the food during cooking. They can melt into a big bright-colored blob.

- Best Sauces I know are made with unsalted butter and evaporated milk.

- Basic White Sauce can be an overcooked mess. "Smooth" sauce with an electric mixer or blender.

- QUICK CHOCOLATE FONDUE SAUCE: Combine 1 cup semi-sweet chocolate chips, 1 cup miniature marshmallows and 1/4 cup milk. Microwave on High 3 to 4 minutes until boiling rapidly. Stir frequently. Makes 1 cup.

BASIC WHITE SAUCE

POWER LEVEL: HIGH   SERVES: 1 cup
TOTAL COOKING TIME: 3 to 4-1/2 minutes

Thin Sauce:

    1 Tbsp. butter or margarine
    1 Tbsp. all-purpose flour
    1/4 tsp. salt
    1 cup milk

Medium Sauce:

    2 Tbsp. butter or margarine
    2 Tbsp. all-purpose flour
    1/4 tsp. salt
    1 cup milk

Microwave butter in 1-quart casserole or measure for 30 seconds to 1 minute on High. Stir in flour and salt until smooth. Slowly blend in milk, sitrring constantly. Microwave on High 2-1/2 to 3-1/2 minutes. Stir every minute to prevent lumping.

VARIATIONS:

MORNAY SAUCE: Add 1/2 cup shredded swiss, gruyere or Parmesan cheese, 1 tsp. lemon juice and a dash of cayenne pepper to hot cooked white sauce. Stir well.

CHEESE SAUCE: Add 1/2 cup grated Cheddar cheese and 1/2 tsp. dry mustard to hot cooked white sauce. Stir well.

MUSTARD SAUCE: Add 1 Tbsp. horseradish and 1-1/2 tsp. dry mustard to hot cooked white sauce.

BASIC GRAVY

POWER LEVEL: HIGH   SERVES: 1-1/2 cups
TOTAL COOKING TIME: 5 to 7 minutes

1/3 to 1/2 cup pan drippings
1/4 cup flour
1/4 tsp. salt
1-1/4 cups water, milk or half and half

Place drippings in a 1-quart measure or casserole.
Microwave on High for 45 seconds to 1 minute until
bubbly. Stir flour and salt into drippings. Mix
well. Slowly stir milk into liquid until smooth.
Microwave on High 4 to 6 minutes or until thickened.
Stir every minute to prevent lumps. If desired, add
browning agent for browner gravy.

MUSHROOM SAUCE

POWER LEVEL: MEDIUM HIGH   SERVES: 2 cups
TOTAL COOKING TIME: 6 to 7 minutes

2 cups sliced fresh mushrooms
1/4 cup butter or margarine
1/4 cup water
1/4 cup sherry wine or additional water
1 Tbsp. cornstarch
1/4 tsp. salt

Place mushrooms and butter in a 1-quart casserole.
Cover with waxed paper and Microwave at Medium High
for 3 minutes. Stir together water, sherry, cornstarch and salt. Slowly stir into mushrooms. Cover
with waxed paper and Microwave at Medium High for
3 to 4 minutes or until thick. Stir twice during
cooking.

SPAGHETTI SAUCE

POWER LEVEL: HIGH AND MEDIUM   SERVES: 4
TOTAL COOKING TIME: 18 to 24 minutes

---

1 pound ground beef
1 small onion, chopped
1 clove garlic, chopped
1 stalk celery, chopped
1/2 cup fresh mushrooms, chopped (optional)
1 can (16 oz.) stewed tomatoes
1 can (6 oz.) tomato paste
1 tsp. parsley flakes
1/2 tsp. salt
1/2 tsp. basil
1/2 tsp. oregano
1/4 tsp. pepper

In a 2-quart casserole, place beef, onion, garlic, celery and mushrooms. Microwave on High 4 to 6 minutes. Meat should be slightly pink. Drain and break up beef. Stir in remaining ingredients. Microwave on Medium, covered with waxed paper, for 14 to 18 minutes. Stir twice during cooking. Serve over spaghetti.

BEST BARBECUE SAUCE

POWER LEVEL: HIGH   SERVES: 2 cups
TOTAL COOKING TIME: 5 to 7 minutes

---

1 cup chili sauce   2 Tbsp. prepared mustard
1/2 cup molasses   1/2 tsp. salt
1/2 cup beer or gingerale

Mix all ingredients together in a 1-quart casserole. Cover tightly and Microwave on High 5 to 7 minutes or until hot. Stir halfway through cooking. Excellent when mixed with chipped ham or ground meat for sandwiches.

118

BUTTERSCOTCH SAUCE

POWER LEVEL: HIGH   SERVES: 1-1/2 cups
TOTAL COOKING TIME: 4 to 5 minutes

1-1/4 cups brown sugar
1 Tbsp. cornstarch
1/2 cup dairy half and half
2 Tbsp. light corn syrup
1/8 tsp. salt
1/4 cup butter or margarine
1 tsp. vanilla, rum or maple flavoring

Stir together sugar and cornstarch in a 1-1/2 quart casserole. Stir in half and half, corn syrup and salt. Add butter. Cover with waxed paper. Microwave on High 4 to 5 minutes, until sauce is thickened and sugar is dissolved. Stir twice during cooking. Add flavoring and stir until smooth. Store in refrigerator. Serve warm or cold.

CRANBERRY SAUCE

POWER LEVEL: HIGH   SERVES: 2 to 3 cups
TOTAL COOKING TIME: 10 to 12 minutes

2 cups sugar
1 cup water
1 pound fresh cranberries

In a 3-quart casserole, mix together sugar, water and washed cranberries. Cover tightly. Microwave on High 10 to 12 minutes or until berries pop. Stir after 5 minutes cooking time. Let stand, covered, for 5 to 10 minutes. Serve warm or cold.

VARIATION: Substitute orange juice or pineapple juice for water.

ORANGE AND LEMON BUTTER SAUCE

POWER LEVEL: HIGH   SERVES: 1 cup
TOTAL COOKING TIME: 3 to 4 minutes

1/2 cup sugar
1-1/2 Tbsp. cornstarch
1 to 2 tsp. grated orange or lemon peel
3/4 cup water
1/4 cup orange or lemon juice
2 Tbsp. butter or margarine

In a 1-quart measure or casserole, combine sugar, cornstarch, peel, water and juice. Mix well until smooth.
Microwave on High 3 to 4 minutes, stirring every minute
to prevent lumping. Stir in butter. Serve with cake,
ice cream, fruit and pudding.

* JAMS AND JELLIES *

° Jams and jellies are excellent in the microwave as they retain fresh flavor and bright color.

° Fruit juices do not evaporate so powder or liquid pectin is needed for consistent results.

° Liquid pectin is added with sugar. Powdered pectin is boiled with the fruit so it dissolves before the sugar is added.

° DO NOT DOUBLE A MICROWAVE JELLY OR JAM RECIPE. TIMING MAY NOT BE ACCURATE.

° An _advantage_ of a microwave jam and jelly making is "no scorching".

° A _disadvantage_ is frequent boil-overs. (Start in a very large container that has at least 4 cups extra boiling space).

° Place a paper towel under the jam or jelly container. If it boils over, the clean up is easy.

° TEST FOR DONENESS. Dip a large metal spoon into the boiling syrup. The jelling point is reached when the syrup runs off the spoon in a sheet.

° STERILIZING SHOULD BE DONE ON A REGULAR RANGE TOP.

Gift Hint. Place a washed bunch of grapes in each glass before adding jelly. Use within 2 weeks as grapes will begin to age.

FROZEN STRAWBERRY JAM

POWER LEVEL: HIGH   SERVES: 3-1/2 to 4 cups
TOTAL COOKING TIME: 22 to 26 minutes

2 packages (16 oz. each) frozen strawberries, thawed
1 package (1-3/4 oz.) powdered pectin
2-1/2 cups sugar
1 Tbsp. lemon juice

Place strawberries and pectin in a 3-quart casserole.
Stir well. Crush fruit, if desired. Cover with
plastic wrap. Microwave on High for 10 to 12 minutes,
until mixture comes to a full boil. Stir twice during
cooking. Stir in sugar and lemon juice and mix well.
Microwave at High, uncovered, for 12 to 14 minutes.
Mixture should boil rapidly for 1 to 2 minutes. Skim
off foam. Cool for 5 to 7 minutes, stirring well.
Ladle into sterilized jars and seal. Refrigerate for
2 to 3 weeks or freeze up to 1 year.

VARIATIONS: Substitute frozen peaches or other berries
             for strawberries.

GRAPE JELLY FROM FROZEN JUICE

POWER LEVEL: HIGH   SERVES: 1 quart
TOTAL COOKING TIME: 16 to 18 minutes

1 can (6 oz.) frozen grape juice
1 package (1-3/4 oz.) powdered fruit pectin
2 cups hot water
3-3/4 cups sugar

Place grape juice, pectin, and hot water in a 3-quart
casserole. Cover tightly and Microwave on High 10 minutes or until mixture boils rapidly. Stir twice during
cooking. Add sugar and stir until dissolved. Cover and
Microwave on High for 6 to 8 minutes or until mixture
boils rapidly for 1 to 2 minutes. Skim off foam. Pour
into sterilized jars. Seal. Refrigerate for 2 to 3
weeks or freeze up to a year.

* BROWNING DISH *

° Two types of browning dishes are available on the market. A browning griddle is a flat dish with a well around the outside to catch drippings. It gives a large browning surface but has no lid. The second model is a browning dish with sides and a lid. It is handy for browning meat to which other ingredients will be added for a casserole. The lid controls splattering and moisture.

° A browning dish can be used as a regular microwave casserole as long as the bottom of the dish is covered with food. DO NOT USE A BROWNING DISH IN A CONVENTIONAL OVEN OR RANGE TOP.

* * * WARNING * * *

At maximum microwave absorption, the dish attains a temperature of 500°F to 600°F. Do not cover the dish with paper products or place a preheated browning dish on a counter.

° Lightly butter the food or use a non-stick vegetable oil so food will not stick. Butter and oil are added to the preheated dish.

° Preheating time depends on the type of food. Do not preheat the dish more than 8 minutes, it could crack.

° Clean with soda, a plastic scouring pad or put the dish in the dishwasher.

BROWNING DISH AND GRILL IDEAS

FRIED TOMATOES — Dip sliced tomatoes in crushed corn flake crumbs. Preheat browning dish or grill 5 minutes on High. Brown 1 minute on each side.

HASH BROWN
POTATOES — Preheat browning dish or grill 5 minutes on High. Add 1 Tbsp. butter or margarine to dish. Add a medium size bag of shredded hash brown potatoes, thawed, to the hot dish. Sprinkle with paprika. Microwave 4 to 6 minutes, stirring every 2 minutes.

FROZEN PIZZA — Preheat browning dish or grill 5 minutes on High. Place 4 frozen pizza slices on hot dish and Microwave for 3 to 5 minutes or until cheese is bubbly near the center. Do not overcook.

QUICK HASH
AND EGG NESTS — for lunch and breakfast -- Preheat browning dish or grill 5 minutes on High. Add 1 Tbsp. butter or margarine to grill. Spoon hash onto dish in 4 patty shapes. Indent each patty deep enough for an egg in the center. Place a broken egg into each patty. Sprinkle with salt and pepper. Microwave on High 6 to 8 minutes until eggs are done.

GRILLED FRUIT
IN BUTTERSCOTCH
SAUCE — is delicious and easy. Dip sliced and peeled apples, bananas or fresh pineapple into melted butter and a mixture of granulated sugar and cinnamon. Preheat grill or dish for 5 minutes on High. Brown fruit pieces 1 minute on each side. Serve with Butterscotch Sauce page 119 or Orange Sauce page 120.

RECIPE FOR BROWNING GRILL

GRILLED LAMB PATTIES

POWER LEVEL: HIGH   SERVES: 4
TOTAL COOKING TIME: 5 to 6 minutes

1 pound lean ground lamb   1/2 tsp. garlic salt
1 tsp. instant minced onion   1/4 tsp. cinnamon
1/4 cup dry bread crumbs   1/2 tsp. curry powder
1/3 cup raisins or currants   1 egg
1 cup (8 oz.) plain yogurt

Combine all ingredients except yogurt. Divide mixture into 4 patties 1/2 inch thick. Preheat browning
grill or dish for 8 minutes on High. Place patties
on hot grill. Microwave on High for 3 minutes on
one side. Turn over and cook 2 to 3 minutes. Serve
with yogurt.

RECIPE FOR BROWNING GRILL

GRILLED CHEESE SANDWICHES

POWER LEVEL: HIGH   SERVES: 4 sandwiches
TOTAL COOKING TIME: 2 to 3 minutes

8 slices bread
4 slices cheese
1/4 cup butter or margarine, softened

Place cheese in bread, making 4 sandwiches. Lightly
spread butter on outside of bread. Preheat browning
grill for 5 minutes. Place sandwiches on hot dish.
Microwave 1 minute on High. Turn over and continue
cooking 1 to 2 minutes. Let sandwiches remain on
grill 1 to 2 minutes to finish toasting.

RECIPE FOR BROWNING GRILL

MEAT SHISH-KABOB'S

POWER LEVEL: HIGH   SERVES: 4
TOTAL COOKING TIME: 5 to 6 minutes

---

1 pound lean, tender beef or lamb,
  cut in 1 inch cubes
8 to 12 cherry tomatoes
8 to 12 fresh mushrooms or
1/4 inch slices zucchini
4 wooden skewers
1/2 cup soy sauce or salad dressing

Thread meat and vegetables alternately on wooden
skewers, beginning and ending with meat. Marinate
kabobs in sauce or dressing for 1 to 2 hours, covered.
Preheat browning grill for 8 minutes on High. Drain
kabobs and place on hot dish with meat resting on
grill surface. Microwave 2 minutes on High; turn
each kabob over and continue cooking for 3 to 4 minutes until meat is done. Do not over-cook.

RECIPE FOR BROWNING DISH WITH LID

EGGPLANT ITALIANO

POWER LEVEL: HIGH   SERVES: 4
TOTAL COOKING TIME: 10 to 11 minutes

1/2 large eggplant, peeled and sliced 1/2 inch thick
1 egg, beaten
3/4 cup seasoned Italian bread crumbs
1 can (8 oz.) tomato sauce
1/2 tsp. Worcestershire sauce
1/2 tsp. Italian seasonings
1 cup (4 oz.) shredded mozzarella cheese

Dip eggplant slices into egg and coat with crumbs. Preheat browning dish, uncovered, 5 minutes on High. Place slices on preheated dish. Microwave 3 minutes on High. Turn eggplant slices over and cook 2 to 3 minutes more. Combine tomato sauce, Worcestershire sauce and seasonings. Pour over fried eggplant and top with cheese. Cover with glass lid. Microwave 5 minutes on High, until bubbly.

RECIPE FOR BROWNING DISH WITH LID

STEAK ORIENTAL

POWER LEVEL: HIGH   SERVES: 3
TOTAL COOKING TIME: 6 to 9 minutes

---

1 pound tender steak, cut in thin strips
1/2 cup soy sauce
2 Tbsp. honey
1 tsp. ground ginger
1 clove garlic, finely chopped (optional)
2 cups sliced green onions
1 can (5 oz.) water chestnuts, drained
1 tsp. cornstarch
1/4 cup slivered almonds
1 Tbsp. butter or margarine

Combine soy sauce, honey, ginger and garlic in a shallow dish. Add steak, turning to coat in marinade. Cover and marinade in refrigerator 4 to 6 hours or overnight. When ready to cook, drain excess marinade into a medium bowl. Stir vegetables, cornstarch and almonds into marinade. Let stand. Preheat browning dish for 7 minutes on High. Coat preheated dish with butter. Microwave steak for 2 to 4 minutes, until surface is brown but meat is pink inside. Add vegetable mixture. Cover and Microwave on High 4 to 5 minutes until vegetables are tender crisp. Stir twice during cooking.

RECIPE FOR BROWNING DISH WITH LID

BASIC OMELET

POWER LEVEL: HIGH   SERVES: 2
TOTAL COOKING TIME: 2 to 3 minutes

---

4 eggs   Dash of pepper
3 Tbsp. milk   2 Tbsp. butter or margarine
1/4 tsp. salt

Beat together eggs, milk, salt and pepper. Set aside.
Preheat browning dish 3 minutes on High. Add butter
and allow to melt. Pour egg mixture into dish. Cover
with glass lid. Microwave on High for 2 to 3 minutes
until set. Halfway through cooking time loosen omelet from dish. Sprinkle desired filling onto omelet,
loosen edge of omelet from dish, fold in half and
slide into serving dish.

FILLINGS: Sprinkle 1/4 cup grated cheese, 1/4 cup
            diced ham or bacon or 1/4 cup sauteed vege-
            tables onto omelet, if desired.

* MORE "HOT" IDEAS FOR A "COOL" OVEN *

° Don't soak a scorched dish for hours! Fill dish with water, add 2 Tbsp. baking soda and Microwave on High 3 to 6 minutes to remove baked-on food.

° ANIMAL LOVER'S can warm a pet's food for 15 to 30 seconds in a plastic dish.

° Hint for crazy mothers with bored children.

A large bag of marshmallows will entertain children for an hour. Place a few marshmallows in the oven and cook for 2 to 3 minutes. They grow wonderfully plump, 4 times their normal size. Of course, they are overcooked and un-edible but resemble ping-pong balls. They are great fun to throw at each other.

° Warm wet washcloths or compresses on High for 15 to 30 seconds.

° Get as much juice as possible from citrus fruit. Microwave 15 to 30 seconds before cutting and squeezing.

° Soften frozen ice cream for 15 to 20 seconds on High for easy scooping.

° Clarified butter is easy. Microwave 1/2 cup butter in a measuring cup for 2 minutes on High. Clarified layer on top is gently poured into a serving dish.

° Soften hard brown sugar in a box or plastic bag. Add a few drops of water or a piece of apple or bread and Microwave with the box or bag open for 10 to 20 seconds.

° To clarify honey turned to sugar, Microwave on High for 1 to 2 minutes.

* * * WARNING * * *

Do not use glass jars for cooking food in the microwave. Jars can break and explode. Many items can be quickly warmed safely but should not be heated in glass jars over 1 minute. Some baby food manufacturers recommend not warming baby meats and high sugar fruits in the jar for this reason.

The following hints using bottles are safe if carefully timed. Remove all metal lids and trim from bottles.

°   Treat yourself like a princess. Warm hand and face lotion for 15 to 30 seconds.

°   Catsup, syrup or chili sauce won't pour out? Heat bottle for 15 seconds and it will loosen up.

°   Left over catsup or mayonnaise can be turned into a sauce. Add a Tbsp. of orange juice, red wine or butter to the bottle. Heat 45 seconds and shake well.

°   Take the chill off the baby's bottle. Warm for 30 to 45 seconds on High.

°   Plastic lid stuck on a bottle? Microwave on High for 5 to 10 seconds to loosen.

°   Milk frozen? Using defrost, Microwave opened carton or plastic container of frozen milk for 3 to 4 minutes. Let stand 10 minutes and stir.

°   A crafty idea for quick glue drying! Freshly glued paper and wood projects can be dried by microwaving on High for 1 to 2 minutes. Follow time instruction carefully. Paper, wood and dried flowers could burn if overheated.

°   Soften clay by wrapping it in a wet towel and Microwave on High for 2 to 4 minutes. Turn twice during heating.

130

* HAPPY HOLIDAY DOUGH ART *

° HAPPY HOLIDAY DOUGH ART for ornaments, jewelry and pictures. In a large bowl, blend 4 cups flour, 1 cup of salt and 1-1/2 cups hot water. Knead like bread on a lightly floured surface until smooth. Add food coloring, if desired. Roll dough 1/4 to 1/2 inch thick and shape with cookie cutters or knife. Pierce holes in each ornament with a needle to release steam. Place a small hole in ornaments that will be hanging. Arrange 6 to 8, in a circle, on paper towels covering a piece of cardboard. Microwave on Defrost or 30% power for 1-1/2 minute per piece. Turn cardboard 1/4 turn halfway through cooking. Ornaments should appear dry. Cool and brush with a shellac glaze before and after painting. Handle with care when removing dough art from the microwave. It gets very hot. Refrigerate extra dough for a week or two in a plastic container.

* MICROWAVE FLOWER DRYING *

° Flower drying can be done in the microwave on a small scale. A few flowers can be dried at a time. The method takes practice.

° Use silica gel or kitty litter for best results. Dry flowers in a box, pie plate or individual custard cups.

° Choose flowers that are firm, cool and dry, sturdy and not in full bloom. Over-ripe blooms tend to lose their petals when dried.

° Experiment with the most successful flowers first. Try carnations, daisies and daffodils. Stay away from magnolias, dahlias and chrysanthemums which do not dry well. Yellow flowers retain color but white tend to become grey. Bright red color usually darkens and blue flowers turn a purple shade.

* INSTRUCTIONS FOR FLOWER DRYING *

Pour 2 inches of kitty litter or silica gel into a container. Place flowers, with short stems, right side up and evenly spaced into gel. Gently sift the drying agent over flowers until completely covered. Place a 1 cup measure of water in the back of the microwave. Place flower dish or dishes near the center. Heat on High 30 seconds to 3 minutes depending on the number of flowers. Let flowers stand in container for 30 minutes as flowers will continue to dry for 10 to 15 minutes after heating time. Remove a little of the gel and check flowers for dryness. If not dry, re-cover and put back in the microwave for a minute or two. Gently remove flowers and store in a metal or plastic container. Sprinkle flowers with a small amount of drying agent when storing for increased dryness, if desired.

Index

Recipes Listed by Menu Category

EGGS AND CHEESE

VEGETABLES

PASTA AND RICE

BREAD AND MUFFINS

CAKES

COOKIES

DESSERTS

PIES

CANDY

FRUITS

CHRISTA CRAIG

Home Economist
Graduate of Pennsylvania State University

She has been active in the field of home economics and consumer service for many years. Mrs. Craig is a Microwave lecturer and teacher. She serves as a home economics representative for major appliance manufacturers and as a Microwave consultant.

THE MICROWAVE HINT BOOK
c/o Microwave Kitchen
Post Office Box 17466
Pittsburgh, PA   15235

Send to:
Name _____
Street _____
City _____ State _____ Zip _____

_____ Copies. Enclosed please find a check or money
order for $6.95 payable to Microwave Kitchen. Specify
if gift card is to be enclosed.

THE MICROWAVE HINT BOOK
c/o Microwave Kitchen
Post Office Box 17466
Pittsburgh, PA   15235

Send to:
Name _____
Street _____
City _____ State _____ Zip _____

_____ Copies. Enclosed please find a check or money
order for $6.95 payable to Microwave Kitchen. Specify
if gift card is to be enclosed.

THE MICROWAVE HINT BOOK
c/o Microwave Kitchen
Post Office Box 17466
Pittsburgh, PA   15235

Send to:
Name _____
Street _____
City _____ State _____ Zip _____

_____ Copies. Enclosed please find a check or money
order for $6.95 payable to Microwave Kitchen. Specify
if gift card is to be enclosed.